2000-20
BEST POP & MOVIE

TEN YEARS OF SHEET MUSIC HITS!

MW00668307

Produced by
Alfred Music Publishing Co., Inc.
P.O. Box 10003
Van Nuys, CA 91410-0003
alfred.com

Printed in USA.

No part of this book shall be reproduced, arranged, adapted, recorded, publicly performed, stored in a retrieval system,
or transmitted by any means without written permission from the publisher. In order to comply with copyright laws, please apply for
such written permission and/or license by contacting the publisher at alfred.com/permissions.

ISBN-10: 0-7390-7304-4
ISBN-13: 978-0-7390-7304-9

 Alfred Cares. Contents printed on 100% recycled paper.

TABLE OF CONTENTS

ADELIELAND

(from *Happy Feet*)

By John Powell
Arranged by Carol Matz

© 2006 WARNER-OLIVE MUSIC, LLC (ASCAP)
All Rights Administered by UNIVERSAL MUSIC GROUP (ASCAP)
Exclusive Worldwide Print Rights Administered by ALFRED MUSIC PUBLISHING CO., INC.
All Rights Reserved

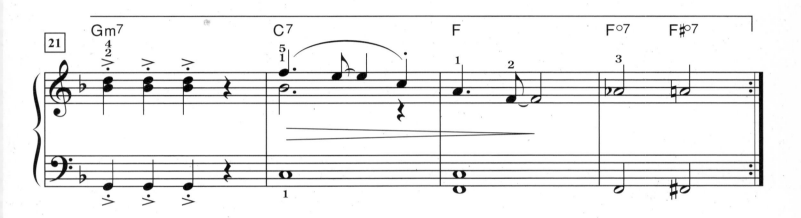

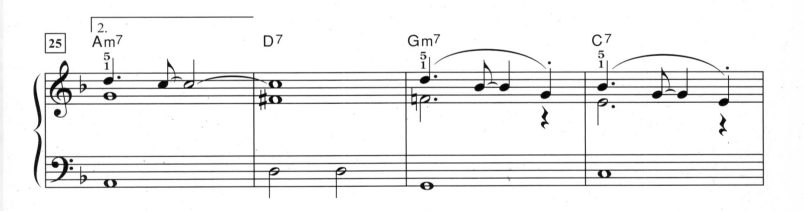

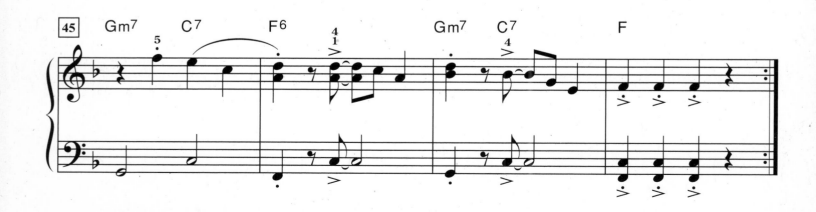

ALL-AMERICAN GIRL

Words and Music by Carrie Underwood,
Kelley Lovelace and Ashley Gorley
Arranged by Carol Matz

© 2007 CARRIE-OKIE MUSIC, DIDN'T HAVE TO BE MUSIC, EMI APRIL MUSIC, INC., SONGS OF COMBUSTION MUSIC
and MUSIC OF WINDSWEPT
All Rights Reserved

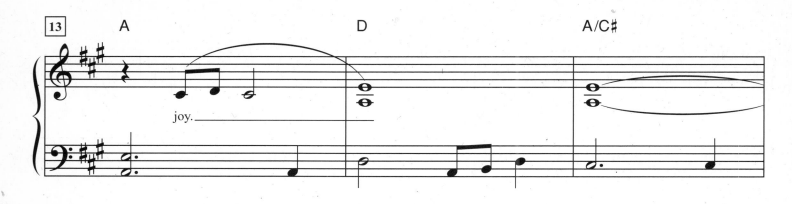

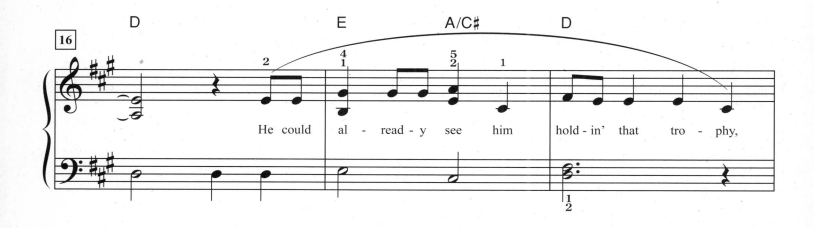

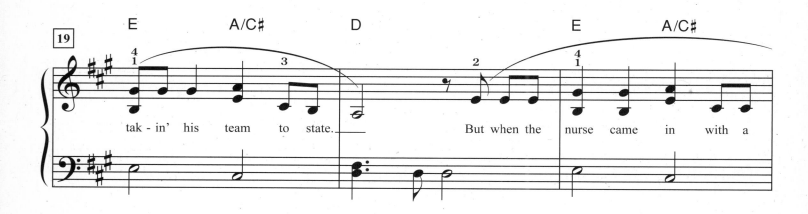

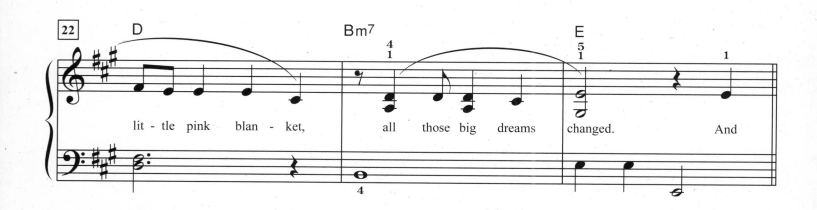

Chorus:

now he's wrapped a-round her fin-ger. She's the cen-ter of his whole world.

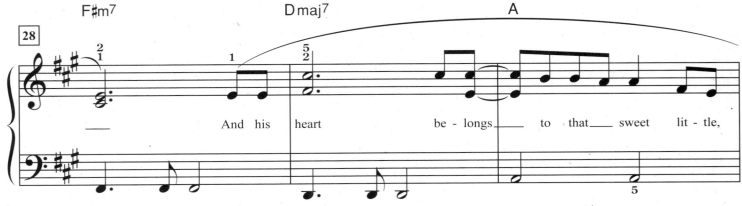

And his heart be-longs to that sweet lit-tle,

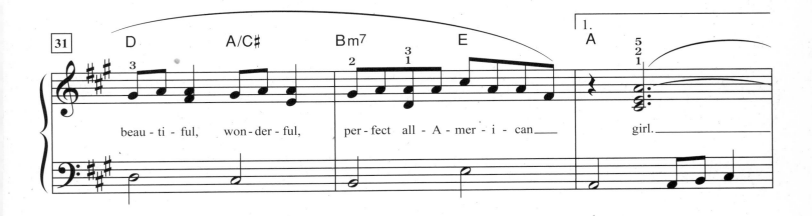

beau-ti-ful, won-der-ful, per-fect all-A-mer-i-can girl.

...and when they got mar-ried and de - cid-ed to have one of their own,

she said, "Be hon-est, tell me what you want." And he said,

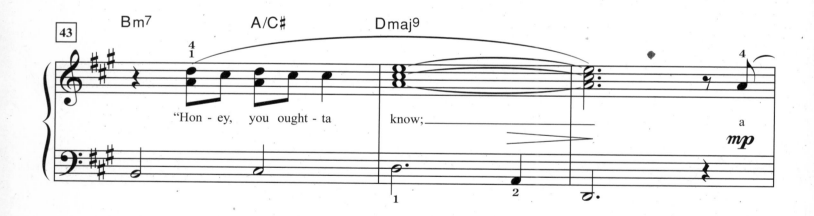

"Hon - ey, you ought - ta know;

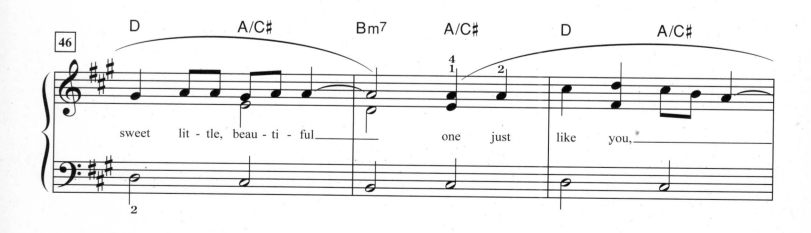

sweet lit - tle, beau-ti-ful one just like you,

Verse 2:
Sixteen short years later,
she was falling for the senior football star.
Before you knew it he was droppin' passes,
skippin' practice just to spend more time with her.
The coach said, "Hey son, what's your problem?
Tell me, have you lost your mind?"
Daddy said, "You'll lose your free ride to college.
Boy, you better tell her goodbye." But…
(Chorus)

AMERICA'S AVIATION HERO

(from *The Aviator*)

By Howard Shore
Arranged by Carol Matz

© 2004 SOUTH FIFTH AVENUE PUBLISHING
All Rights Reserved

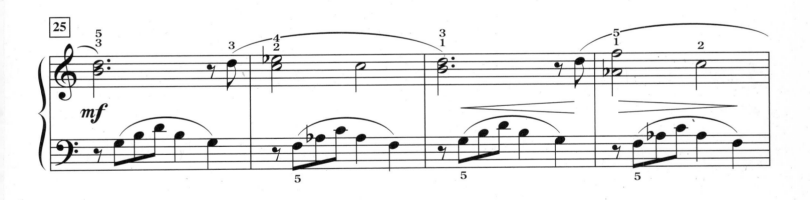

AT LAST

(from *Cadillac Records*)

Music by Harry Warren
Lyrics by Mack Gordon
Arranged by Carol Matz

© 1942 (Renewed) TWENTIETH CENTURY MUSIC CORPORATION
All Rights Controlled by EMI FEIST CATALOG INC. (Publishing) and ALFRED MUSIC PUBLISHING CO., INC. (Print)
All Rights Reserved

My heart was wrapped in clo - ver___ the night I looked at

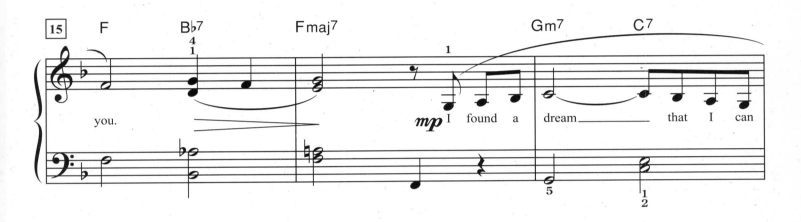

you. *mp* I found a dream___ that I can

speak to, a dream that I can call my own. I found a *mf*

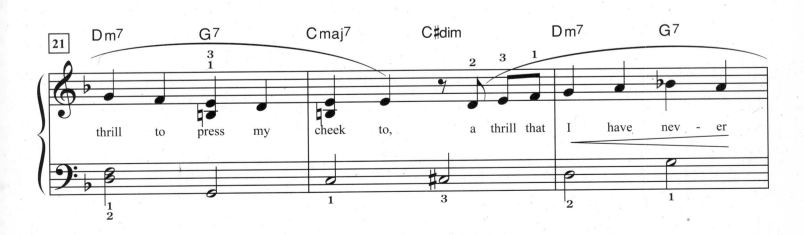

thrill to press my cheek to, a thrill that I have nev - er

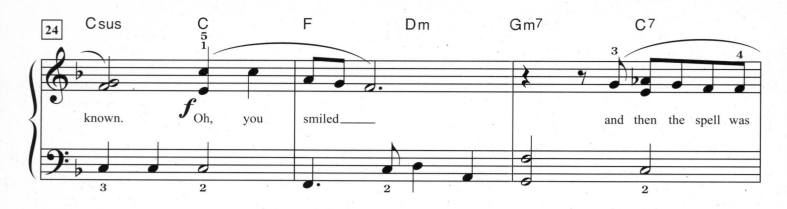

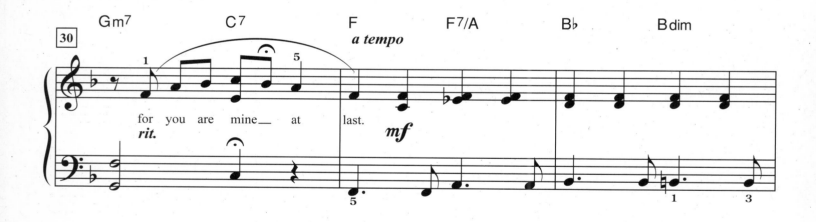

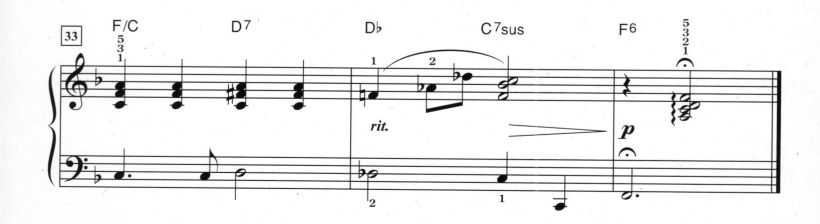

BELIEVE

(from *The Polar Express*)

Words and Music by
Alan Silvestri and Glen Ballard
Arranged by Carol Matz

© 2004 HAZEN MUSIC, JOBANALA MUSIC and AEROSTATION CORPORATION
All Rights for HAZEN MUSIC Administered by WB MUSIC CORP.
All Rights Reserved

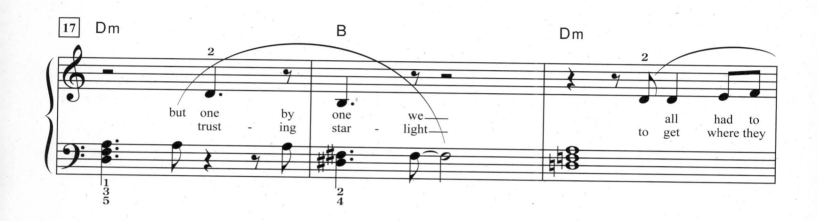

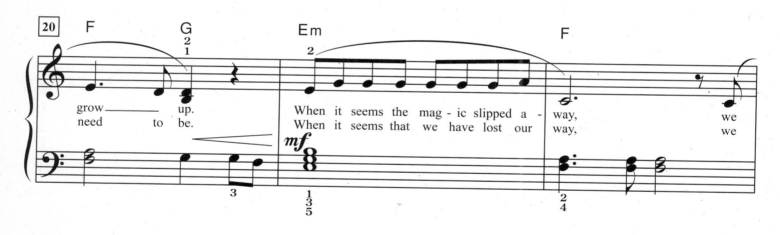

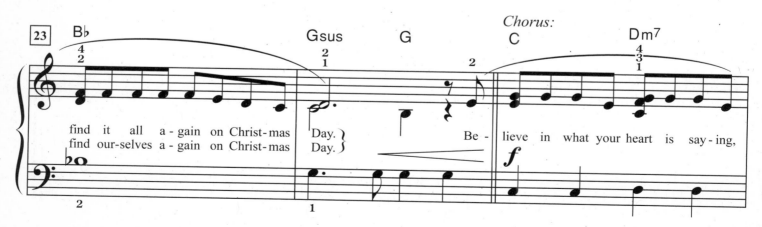

hear the mel - o - dy that's play - ing. There's no time to waste, there's so much to cel - e - brate. Be -

lieve in what you feel in - side and give your dreams the wings to fly.

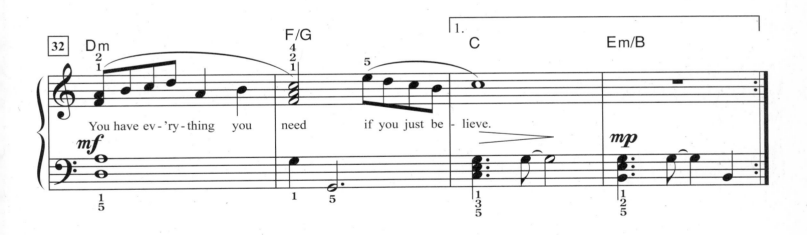

You have ev - 'ry - thing you need if you just be - lieve.

lieve. If you just be - lieve.

molto rit.

BABY

Words and Music by
Terius Nash, Christopher Stewart, Christine Flores,
Christopher Bridges and Justin Bieber
Arranged by Carol Matz

Moderately fast   *Verse:*

1. You know you love me. I know you care. Just shout when-
2., 3. *See additional lyrics.*

ev - er, and I'll be there.__ You want my love,__ you want my

heart, and we will nev - er, ev - er, ev - er be a - part. Are we an

i - tem? Girl, quit play - in'. We're just friends? What are you

© 2009 WB MUSIC CORP., 2082 MUSIC PUBLISHING, SONGS OF PEER LTD., SONGS OF UNIVERSAL INC., HAVANA BROWN PUB-
LISHING, LUDACRIS WORLDWIDE PUBLISHING and JUSTIN BIEBER PUBLISHING DESIGNEE
All Rights on behalf of itself and 2082 MUSIC PUBLISHING Administered by WB MUSIC CORP.
All Rights Reserved

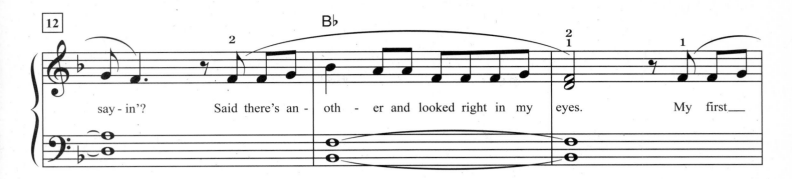

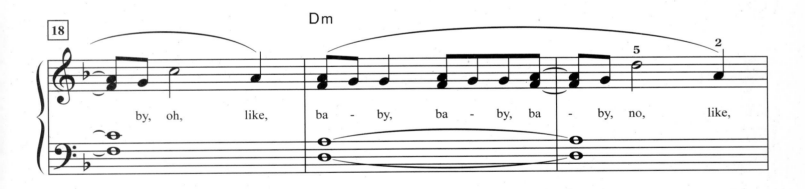

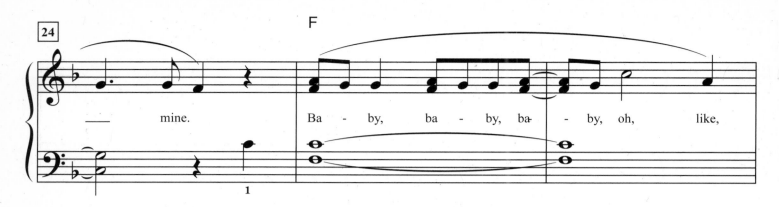

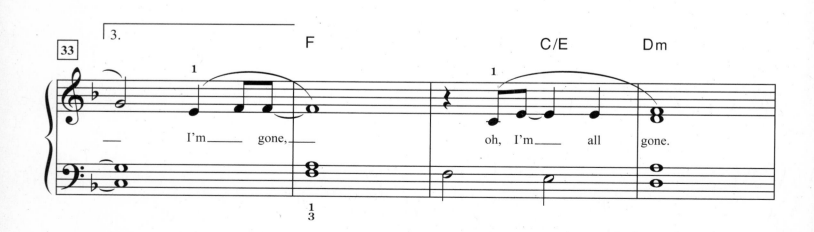

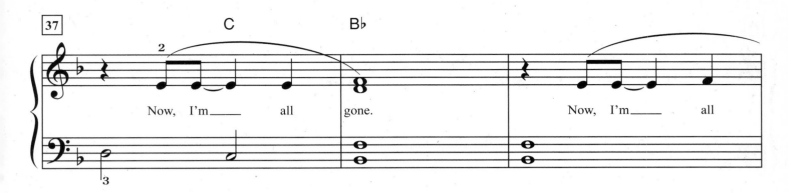

Verse 2:
Oh, for you, I would've done whatever,
And I just can't believe we ain't together.
And I wanna play it cool, but I'm losing you.
I'll buy you anything. I'll buy you any ring.
And I'm in pieces, baby, fix me.
And just shake me till you wake me from this bad dream.
I'm going down, down, down, down.
And I just can't believe my first love won't be around
And I'm like...
(To Chorus:)

Verse 3 Rap:
Luda!
When I was thirteen, I had my first love.
There was nobody that compared to my baby.
And nobody came between us,
Or could ever come above.
She had me going crazy,
Oh, I was starstruck.
She woke me up daily,
Don't need no Starbucks.
She made my heart pound
And skip a beat when I see her in the street,
And at school, on the playground.
But I really wanna see her on a weekend.
She knows she got me dazing,
'Cause she was so amazing.
And now, my heart is breakin',
But I just keep on sayin'...
(To Chorus:)

BELIEVER

(from *Be Cool*)

Words and Music by
Will.I.Am and John Legend
Arranged by Carol Matz

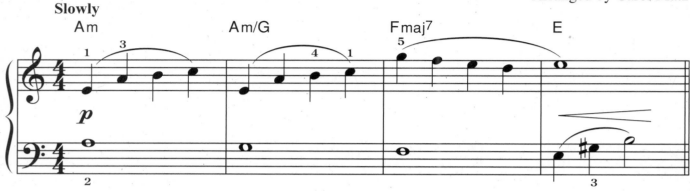

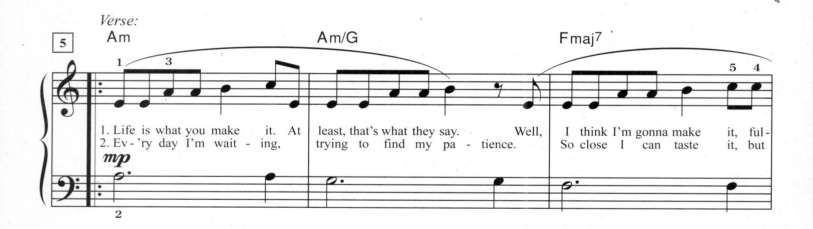

1. Life is what you make it. At least, that's what they say. Well, I think I'm gonna make it, ful-
2. Ev-'ry day I'm wait - ing, trying to find my pa - tience. So close I can taste it, but

fill my dreams one day. I feel this fi - re grow - ing deep in - side of me. I'm
some-times it's so hard. But I'm gon - na keep on push - ing, I'm gonna keep on fight - ing, and

© 2005 UNITED LION MUSIC, INC., CHERRY LANE MUSIC PUBLISHING COMPANY, on behalf of itself and CHERRY RIVER MUSIC CO., WILL.I.AM MUSIC, INC., and JOHN LEGEND PUBLISHING
All Rights Reserved

so in-spir-ed know-ing that it's my des-ti-ny. / I breathe like a cham-pion, I
I'm gonna keep on try-ing, be-cause I've come too far. /

mf

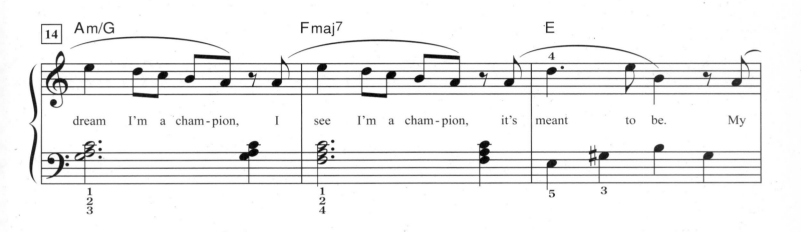

dream I'm a cham-pion, I see I'm a cham-pion, it's meant to be. My

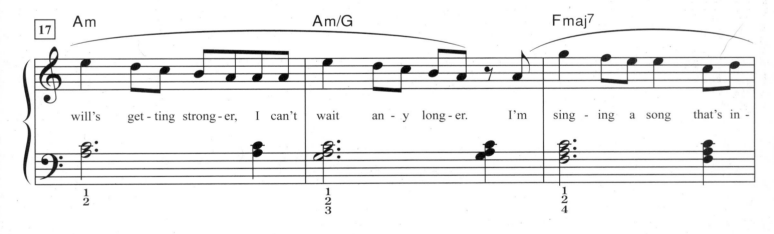

will's get-ting strong-er, I can't wait an-y long-er. I'm sing-ing a song that's in-

Chorus:

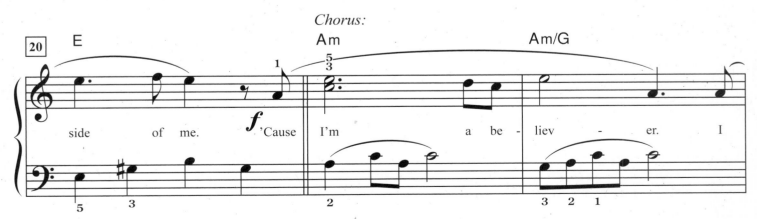

side of me. 'Cause I'm a be-liev-er. I

f

know that I can make it, no mat - ter what they say. I'm a be -

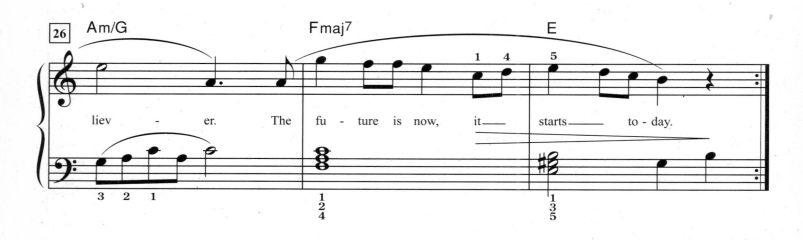

liev - er. The fu - ture is now, it___ starts___ to - day.

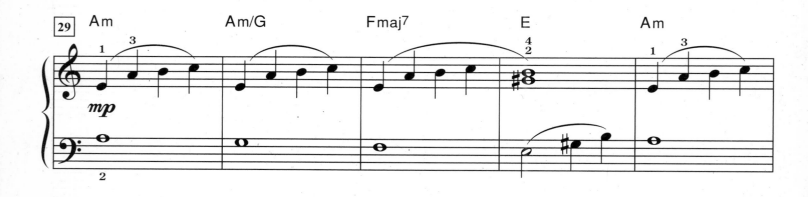

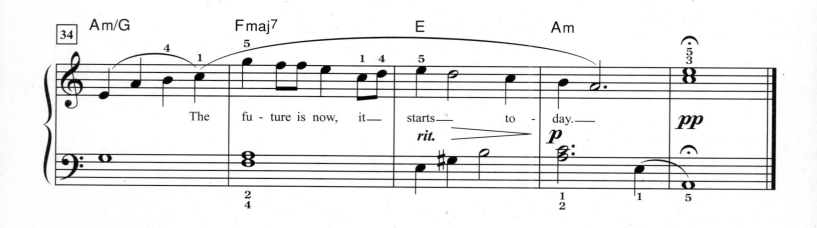

The fu - ture is now, it___ starts___ to - day.___

CALIFORNIA

(from *The O.C.*)

Words and Music by
Al Jolson, B.G. Desylva, Joseph Meyer,
Jason Schwartzman and Alex Greenwald
Arranged by Carol Matz

© 2002 WB MUSIC CORP., JO RO MUSIC CORP., STEPHEN BALLENTINE MUSIC, SHAGSTAR PUBLISHING CO.,
JOHNNY REBEL MUSIC, I LIKE MUSIC, FLYING SAUCER FUEL MUSIC and BEAUCOUP BUCKS MUSIC
{Contains Elements of "CALIFORNIA, HERE I COME" By AL JOLSON, B.G. DESYLVA and JOSEPH MEYER. WB MUSIC CORP.,
LARRY SPIER, INC. o/b/o JORO MUSIC CORP. and STEPHEN BALLENTINE MUSIC}
All Rights Reserved

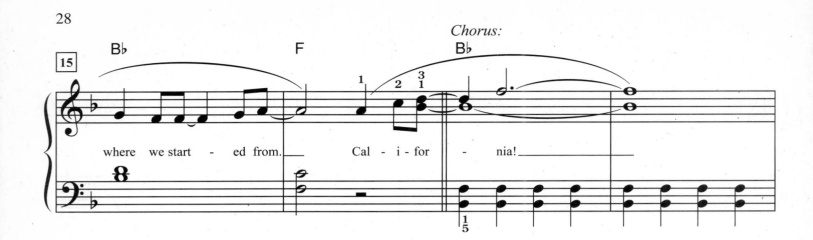

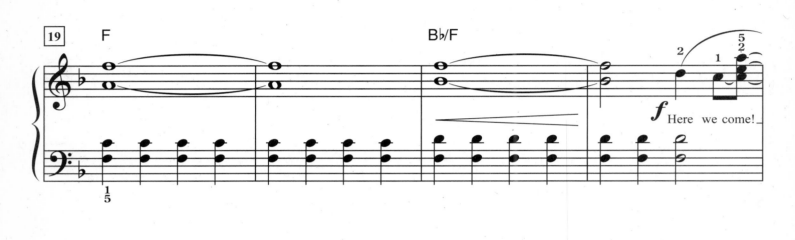

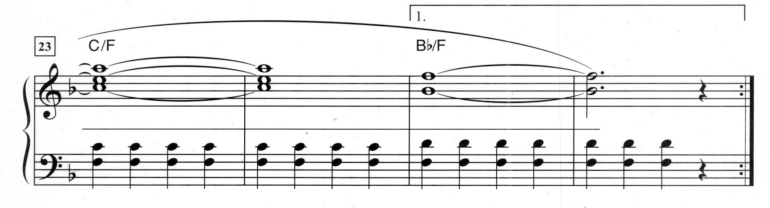

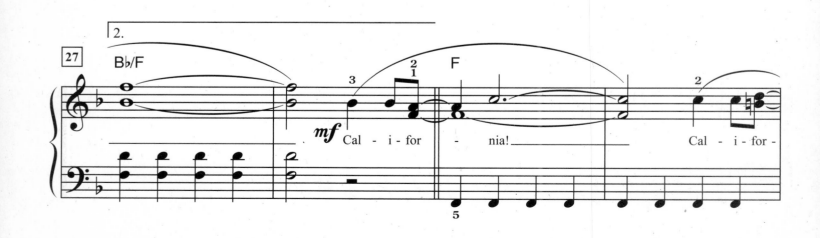

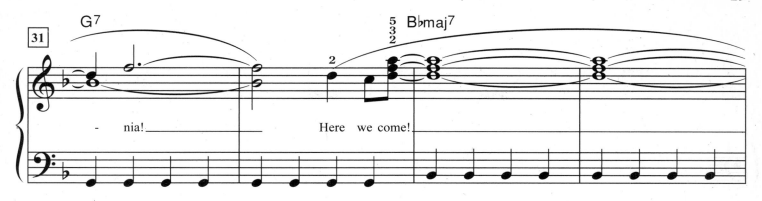

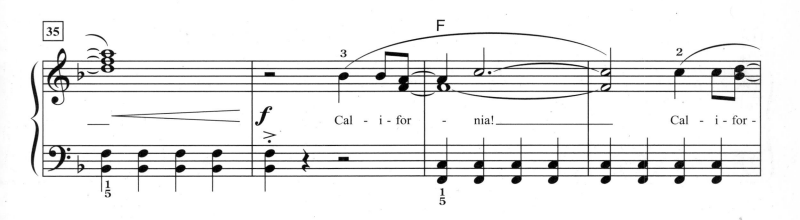

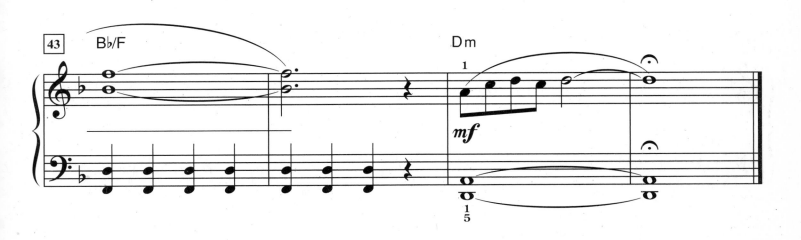

BREAKAWAY

Words and Music by Matthew Gerrard,
Bridget Benenate and Avril Lavigne
Arranged by Carol Matz

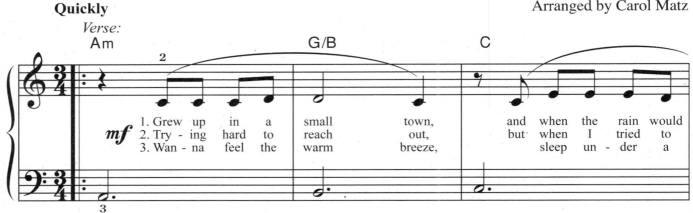

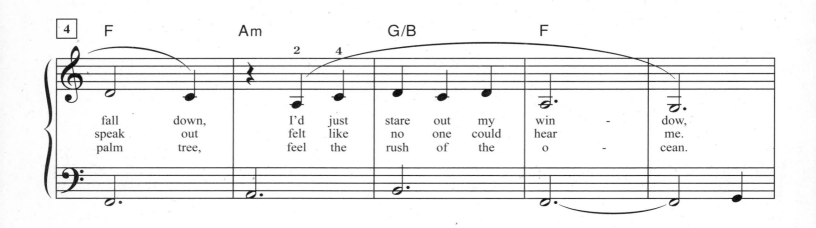

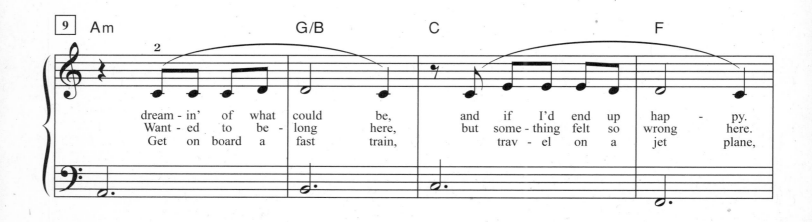

© 2004 WB MUSIC CORP., G MATT MUSIC, WINDSWEPT MUSIC and ALMO MUSIC CORPORATION.
All Rights on behalf of Itself and G MATT MUSIC Administered by WB MUSIC CORP.
All Rights Reserved

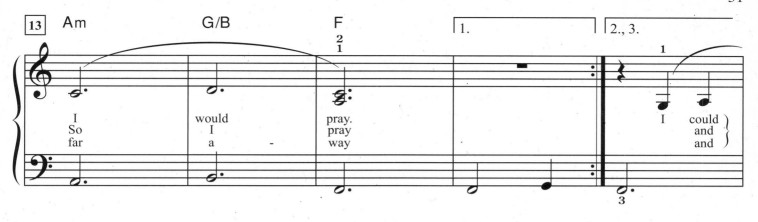

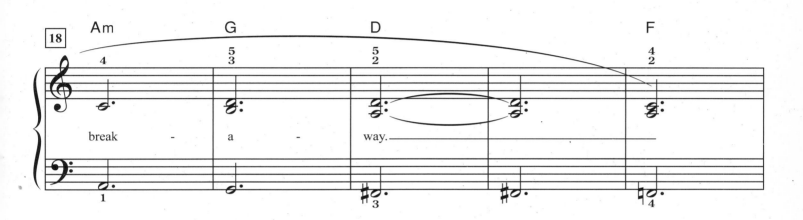

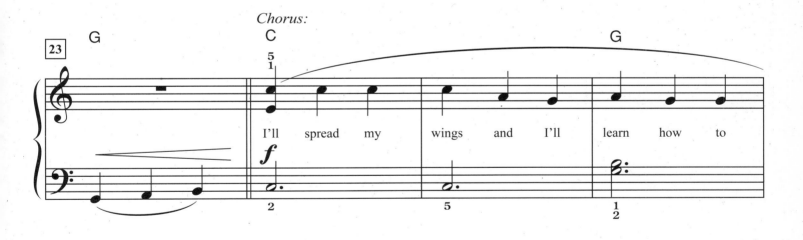

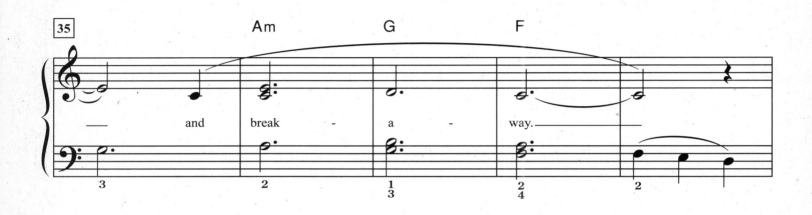

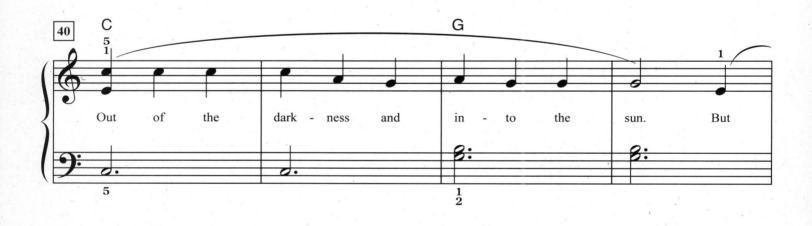

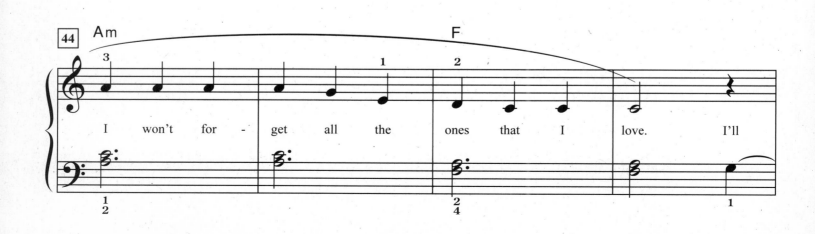

33

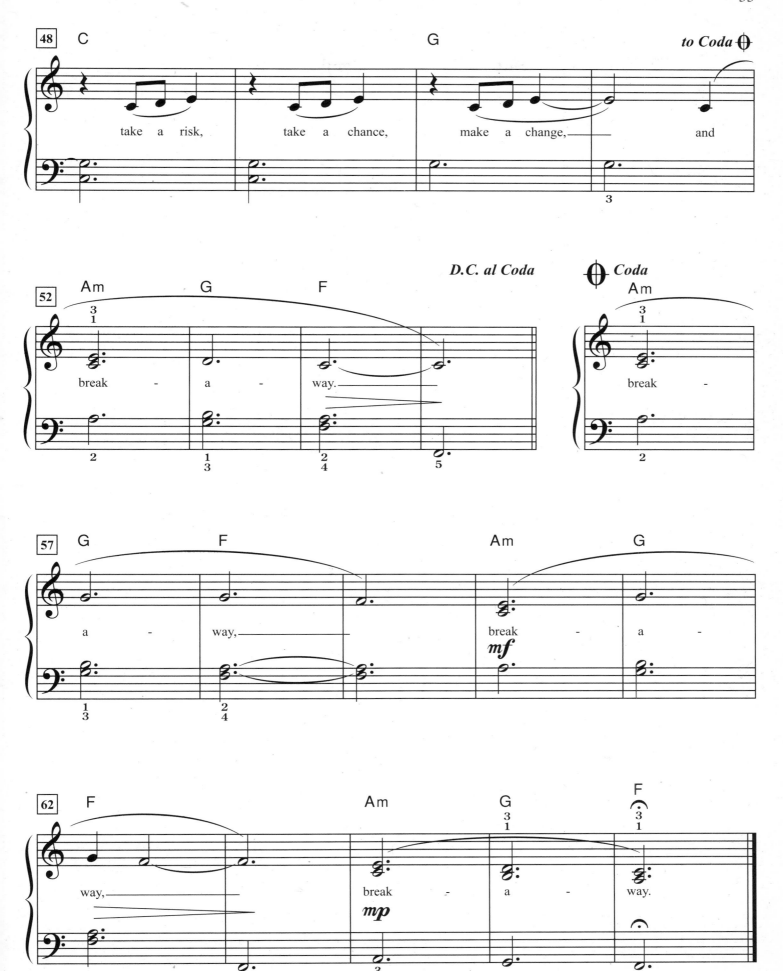

CELEBRATE ME HOME

Lyrics by Kenny Loggins
Music by Kenny Loggins and Bob James
Arranged by Carol Matz

© 1977 (Renewed) MILK MONEY MUSIC
All Rights Reserved

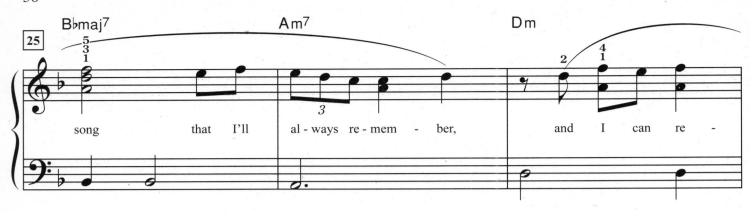

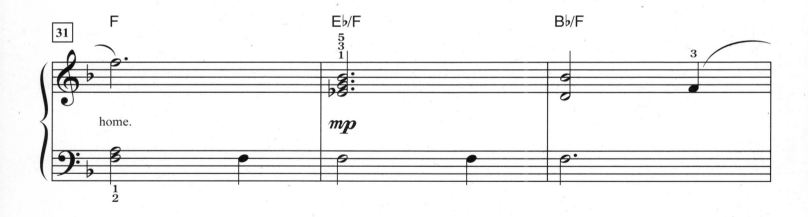

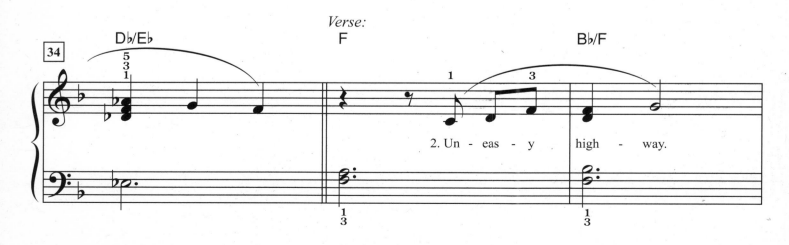

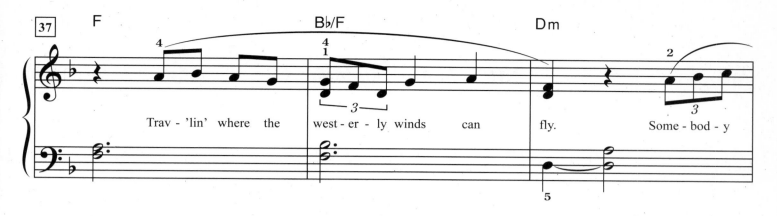

Trav - 'lin' where the west - er - ly winds can fly. Some - bod - y

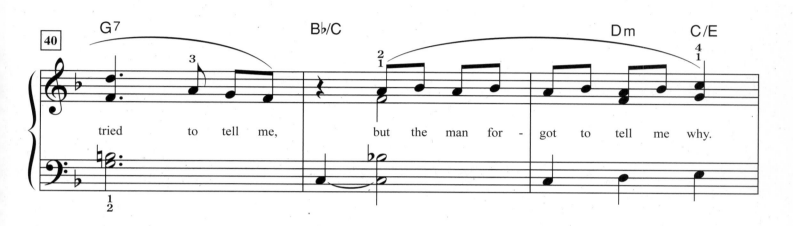

tried to tell me, but the man for - got to tell me why.

I got - ta count on be - ing gone. Come on,___ wom - an,

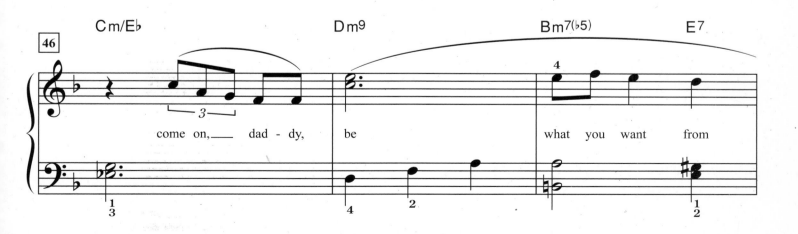

come on,___ dad - dy, be what you want from

CORPSE BRIDE

(Main Title)

Music by Danny Elfman
Arranged by Carol Matz

© 2005 WARNER-BARHAM MUSIC LLC (BMI)
All Rights Administered by SONGS OF UNIVERSAL, INC. (BMI)
Exclusive Worldwide Print Rights Administered by ALFRED MUSIC PUBLISHING CO., INC.
All Rights Reserved

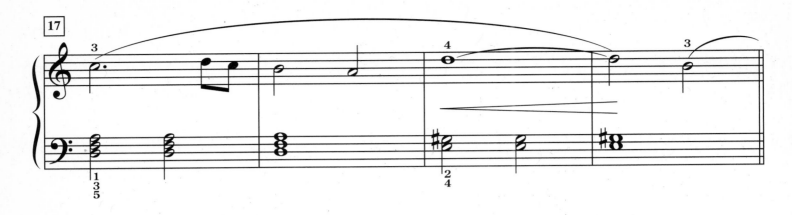

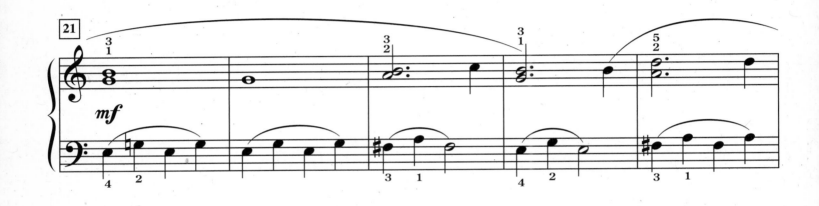

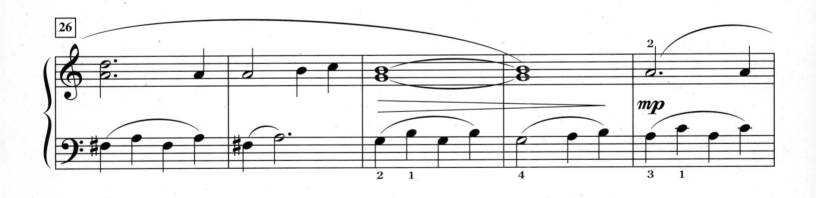

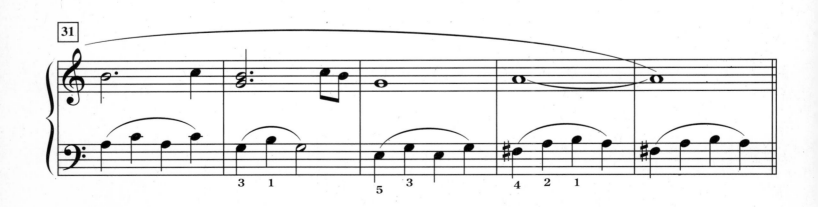

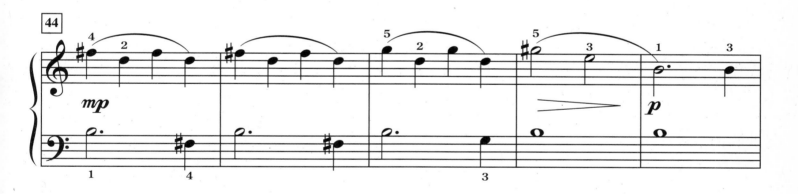

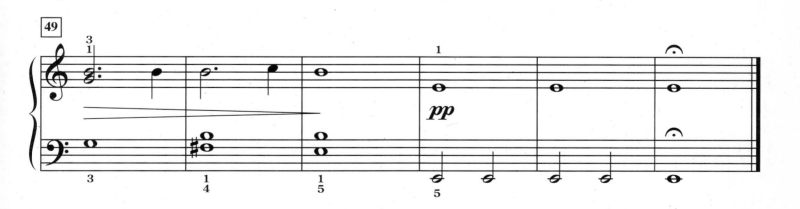

CHARIOT

Words and Music by Gavin Degraw
Arranged by Carol Matz

© 2003 WARNER-TAMERLANE PUBLISHING CORP. (BMI) and G. DEGRAW MUSIC, INC. (BMI)
All Rights Administered by WARNER-TAMERLANE PUBLISHING CORP.
All Rights Reserved

Verse 2:
Remember seeking moon's rebirth?
Rains made mirrors of the earth.
The sun was just yellow energy.
There is a living promised land,
Even over fields of sand.
Seasons fill my mind and cover me.
Bring it back.
More than a memory.

DECODE

(from *Twilight*)

Words and Music by
Hayley Williams, Josh Farro and Taylor York
Arranged by Carol Matz

Moderately
Verse:

1. How can I de-cide what's right___ when you're cloud-ing up my
2. *See additional lyrics.*

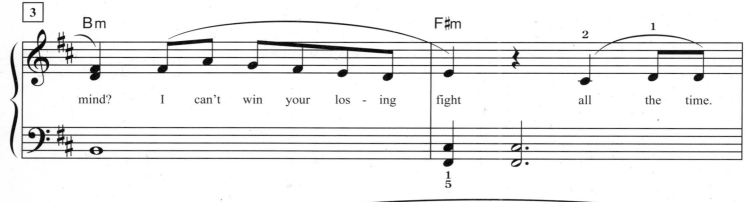

mind? I can't win your los-ing fight all the time.

Nor can I ev-er own what's mine___ when you're al-ways tak-ing

sides. But you won't take a-way my pride, no, not this time.

© 2008 WB MUSIC CORP., BUT FATHER, I JUST WANT TO SING MUSIC, FBR MUSIC, JOSH'S MUSIC,
MEAUX HITS, HUNTERBORO MUSIC, RIMUTAKA MUSIC PUBLISHING and SUMMIT SONGS
All Rights on behalf of itself BUT FATHER, I JUST WANT TO SING MUSIC, FBR MUSIC and JOSH'S MUSIC
Administered by WB MUSIC CORP.
All Rights Reserved

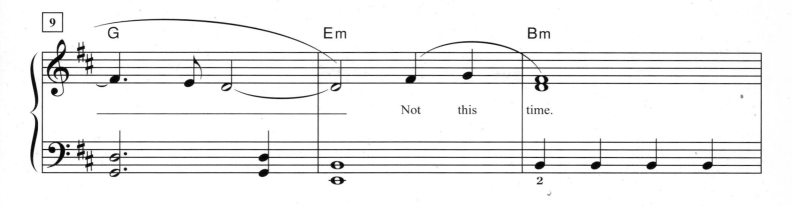

Not this time.

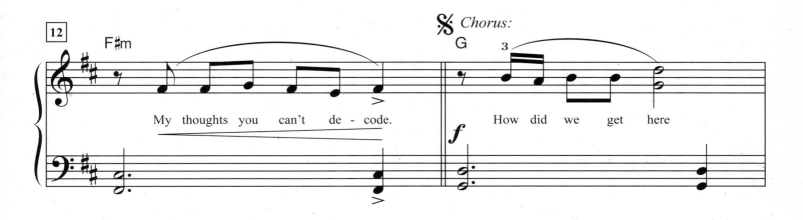

My thoughts you can't de-code.

Chorus:

How did we get here

when I used to know you so well?

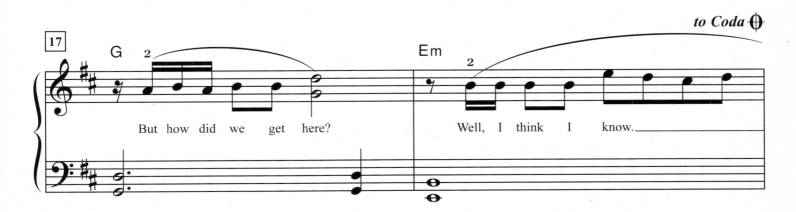

But how did we get here?

Well, I think I know.

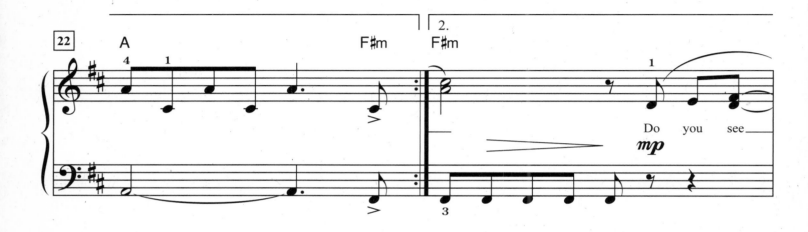

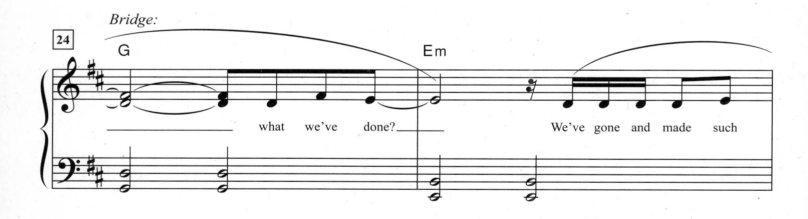

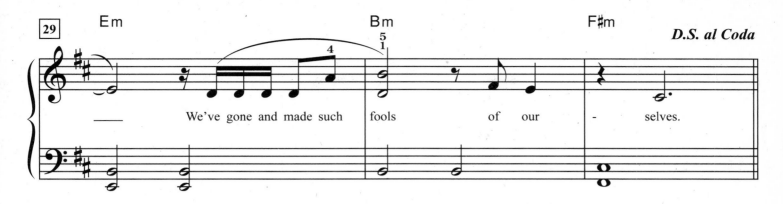

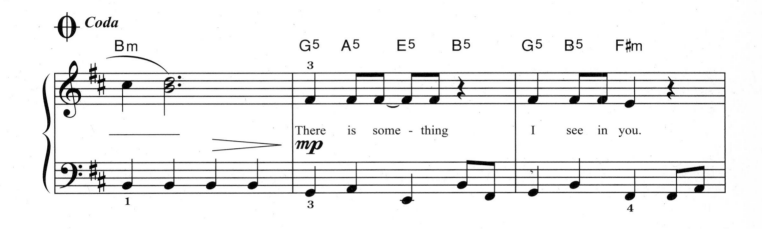

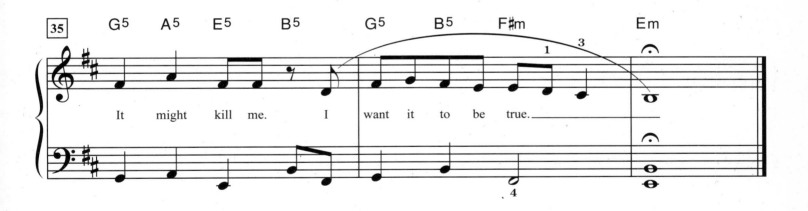

Verse 2:
The truth is hiding in your eyes
And it's hanging on your tongue.
Just boiling in my blood,
But you think that I can't see
What kind of man that you are,
If you're a man at all.
Well, I will figure this one out on my own.
On my own.
(To Chorus)

DON'T STOP BELIEVIN'

(from *Glee*)

Words and Music by
Jonathan Cain, Neal Schon and Steve Perry
Arranged by Carol Matz

© 1981 WEEDHIGH-NIGHTMARE MUSIC and LACEY BOULEVARD MUSIC
All Rights for WEEDHIGH-NIGHTMARE MUSIC Administered by WIXEN MUSIC PUBLISHING INC.
All Rights Reserved

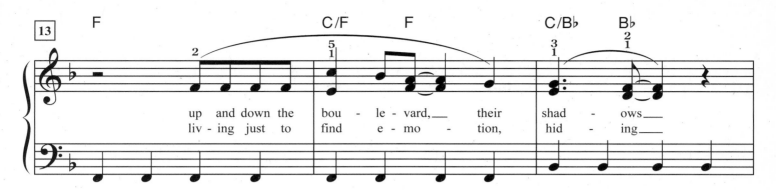

up and down the bou - le - vard,___ their shad - ows___
liv - ing just to find e - mo - tion, hid - ing___

1., 3.

search - ing___ in the night._____

2., 4.

some - where___ in the night.___

to Coda ⊕   *D.C. al Coda*

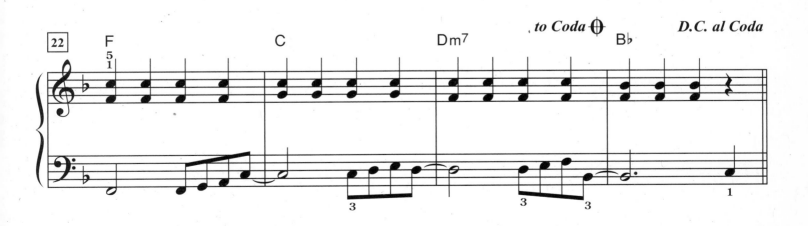

52

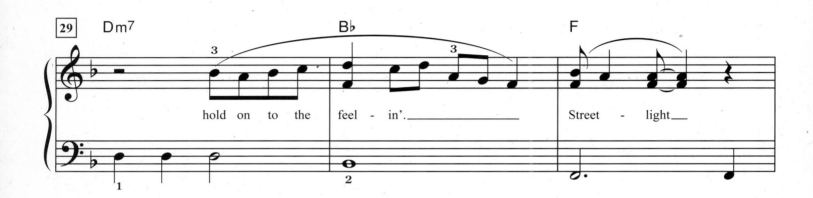

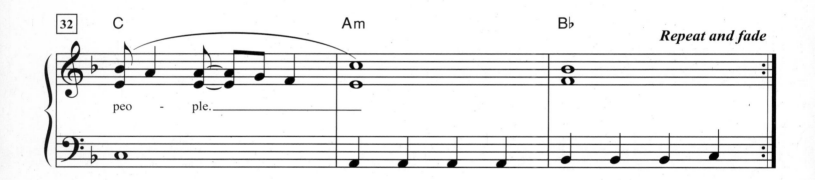

Verse 3:
A singer in a smoky room,
the smell of wine and cheap perfume.
For a smile they can share the night,
it goes on and on and on and on.

Verse 4:
Working hard to get my fill.
Everybody wants a thrill,
payin' anything to roll the dice
just one more time.

Verse 5:
Some will win and some will lose,
some were born to sing the blues.
Oh, the movie never ends,
it goes on and on and on and on.

DOUBLE TROUBLE

(from *Harry Potter and The Prisoner of Azkaban*)

Words and Music by JOHN WILLIAMS
Arranged by Carol Matz

Dou - ble, dou - ble toil and trou - ble; fire_____ burn and caul - dron bub - ble.

Dou - ble, dou - ble toil and trou - ble; some - thing wick - ed this way comes!

Eye of newt and toe of frog,

© 2004 WARNER-BARHAM MUSIC, LLC
All Rights Administered by WARNER-TAMERLANE PUBLISHING CORP.
All Rights Reserved

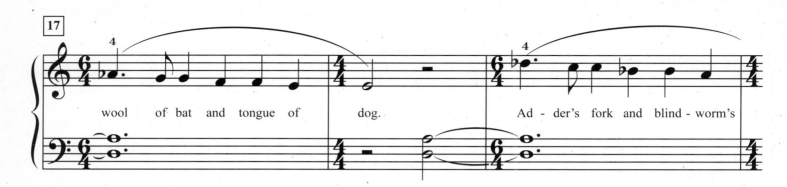

wool of bat and tongue of dog. Ad - der's fork and blind - worm's

sting, liz - ard's leg and owl - et's wing._____

mp

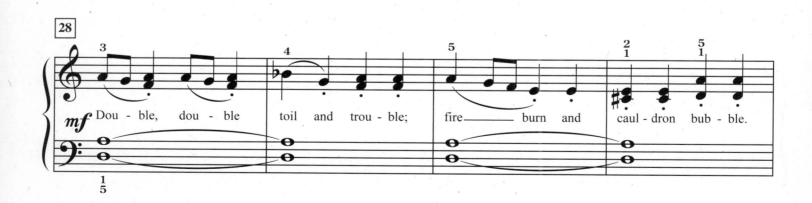

mf Dou - ble, dou - ble toil and trou - ble; fire_____ burn and caul - dron bub - ble.

EVERYTHING

Words and Music by
Michael Bublé, Alan Chang and Amy Foster
Arranged by Carol Matz

© 2006 I'M THE LAST MAN STANDING MUSIC, IHAN ZHAN MUSIC, SONGS OF UNIVERSAL, INC. and ALMOST OCTOBER SONGS
All Rights for I'M THE LAST MAN STANDING MUSIC Administered by WB MUSIC CORP.
All Rights Reserved

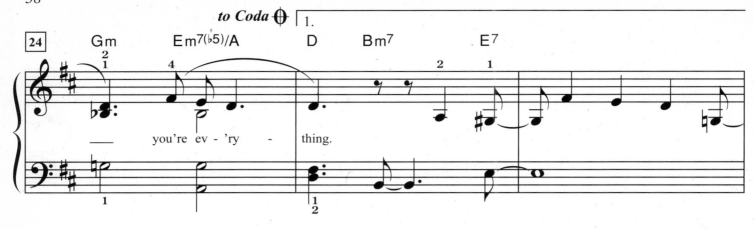

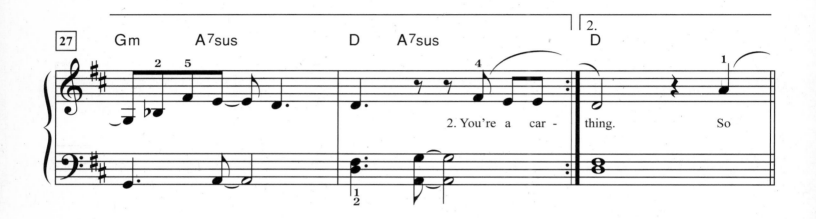

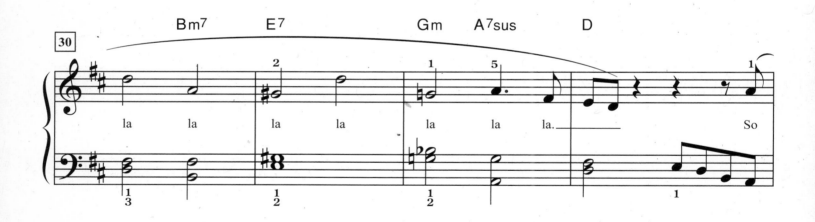

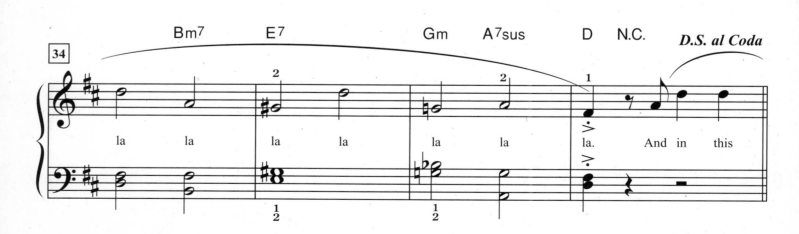

EVERYTHING BURNS

(from *Fantastic Four*)

Words and Music by Ben Moody
Arranged by Carol Matz

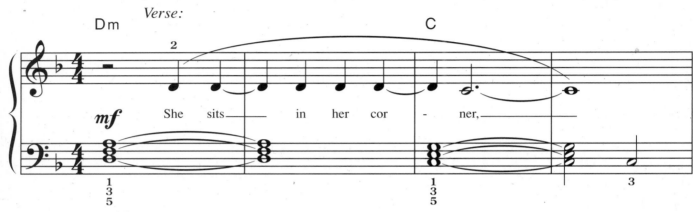

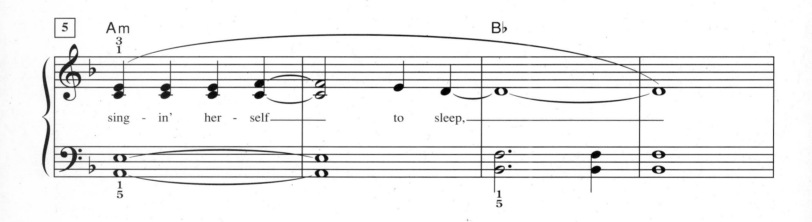

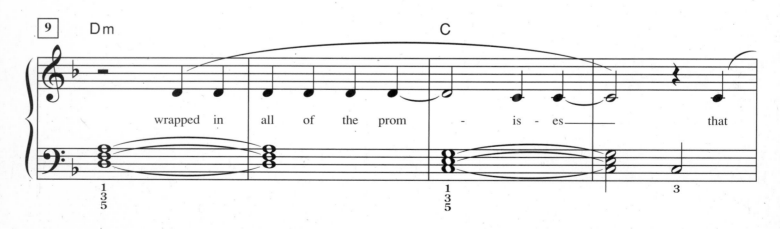

© 2005 SMELLSLIKEMETAL PUBLISHING (BMI) and STATE ONE MUSIC AMERICA (BMI)
All Rights Administered by STATE ONE MUSIC AMERICA (BMI)
All Rights Reserved

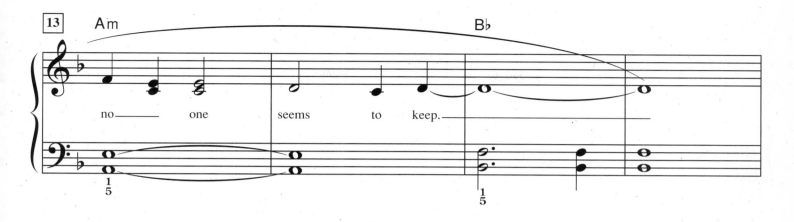

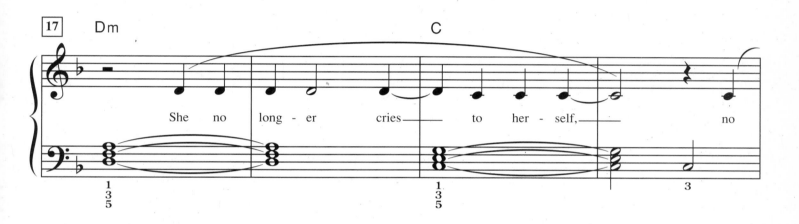

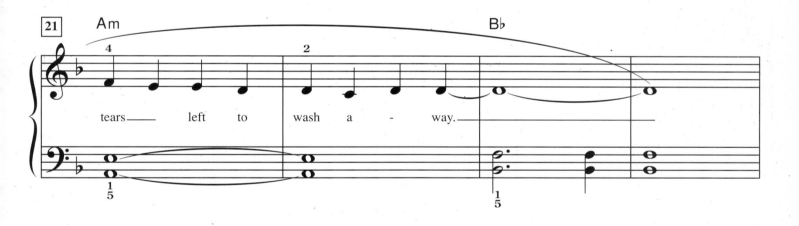

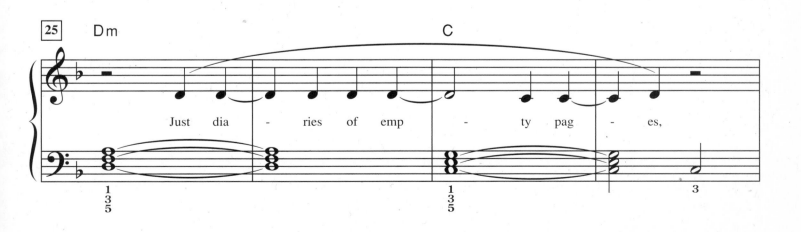

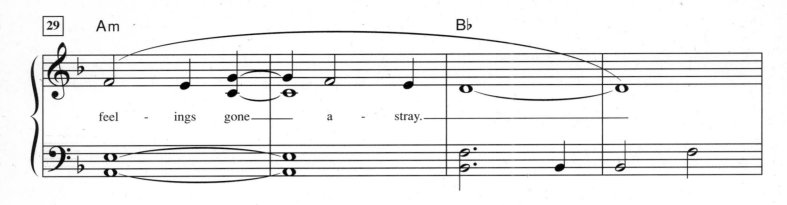

feel - ings gone a - stray.

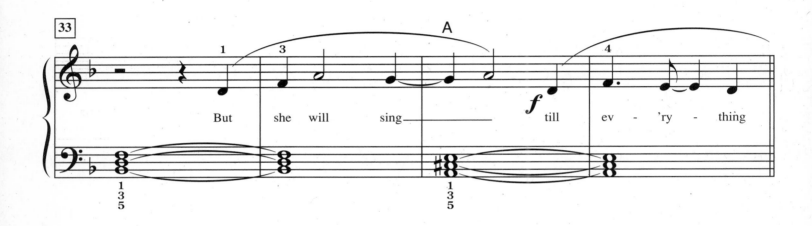

But she will sing till ev - 'ry - thing

Chorus:

burns, while ev - 'ry - one screams, burn - ing their

lies, burn - ing my dreams. All of this

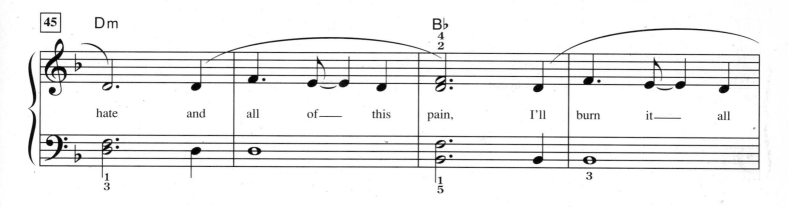

hate and all of — this pain, I'll burn it — all

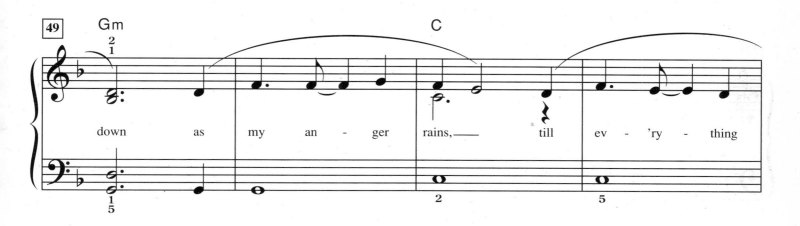

down as my an - ger rains, — till ev - 'ry - thing

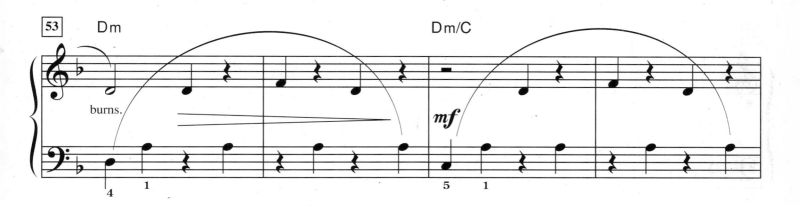

burns.

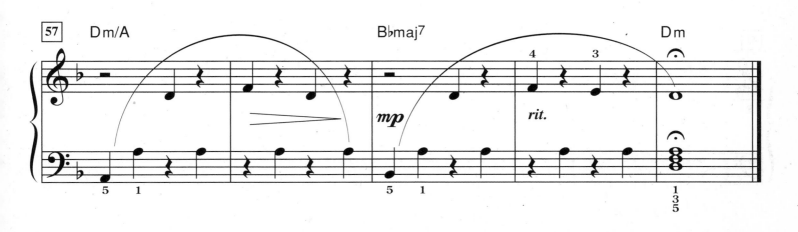

FAWKES THE PHOENIX

(from *Harry Potter and the Chamber of Secrets*)

Music by JOHN WILLIAMS
Arranged by Carol Matz

© 2002 WARNER-BARHAM MUSIC, LLC
All Rights Administered by WARNER-TAMERLANE PUBLISHING CORP.
All Rights Reserved

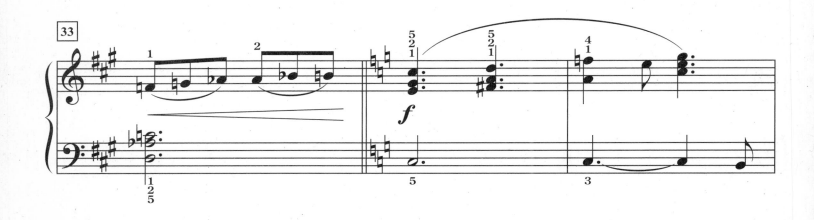

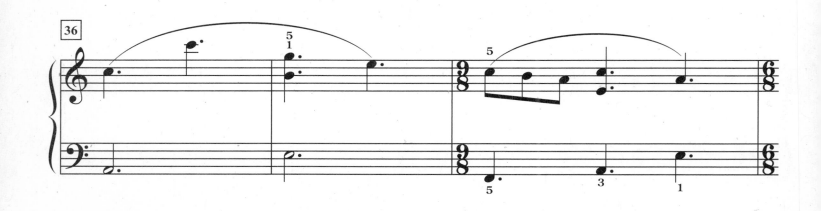

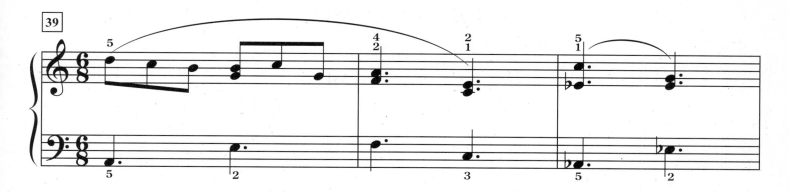

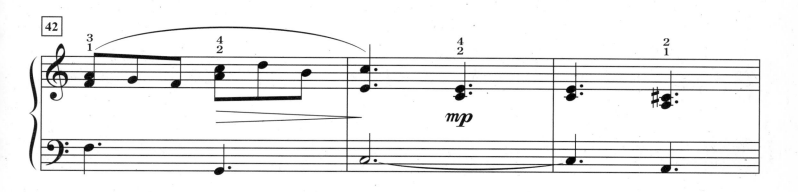

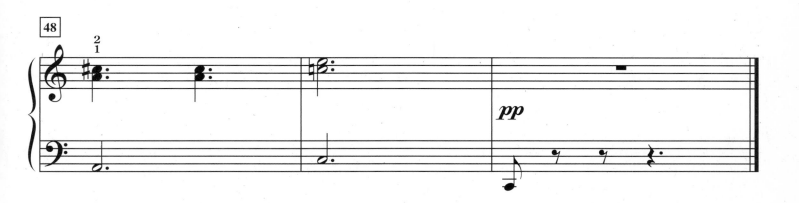

THE GIFT

Words and Music by Jim Brickman and Tom Douglas
Arranged by Carol Matz

© 1997 BRICKMAN ARRANGEMENT/MULTISONGS INC. (SESAC) SONY/ATV TREE PUBLISHING (BMI) and TOMDOUGLASMUSIC (BMI)
Print Rights for BRICKMAN ARRANGEMENT (SESAC) Administered Worldwide by ALFRED MUSIC PUBLISHING CO., INC.
All Rights for SONY/ATV TREE PUBLISHING (BMI) and TOMDOUGLASMUSIC (BMI)
Administered by SONY/ATV MUSIC PUBLISHING, 8 Music Square West, Nashville, TN 37203
All Rights Reserved

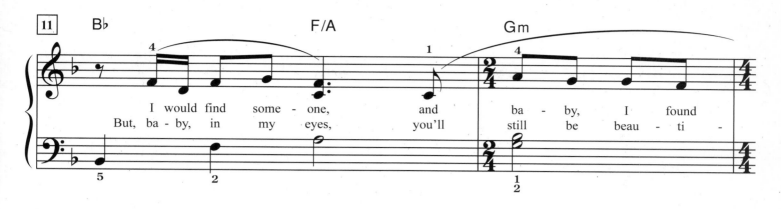

I would find some - one, and ba - by, I found
But, ba - by, in my eyes, you'll still be beau - ti -

Chorus:

you.⎫
ful.⎭ *mf* And all I want is to hold___ you for - ev - er.___ All I

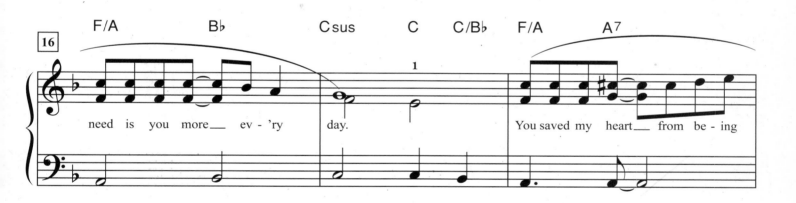

need is you more___ ev - 'ry day. You saved my heart___ from be - ing

to Coda ⊕

bro - ken a - part.___ You gave your love a - way, I'm thank - ful ev - 'ry day for the

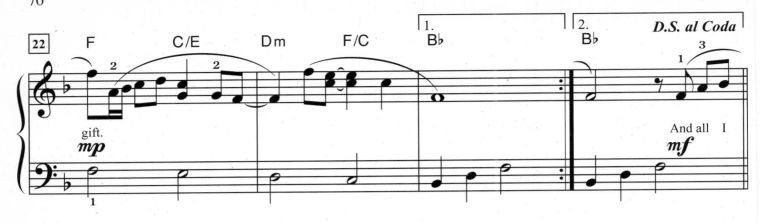

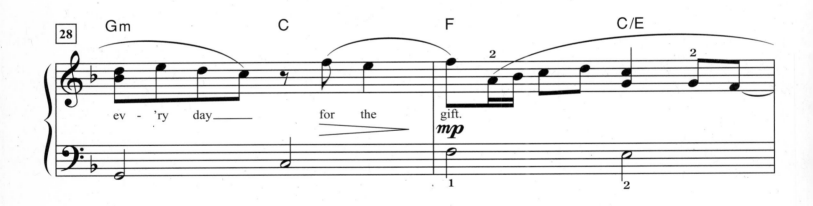

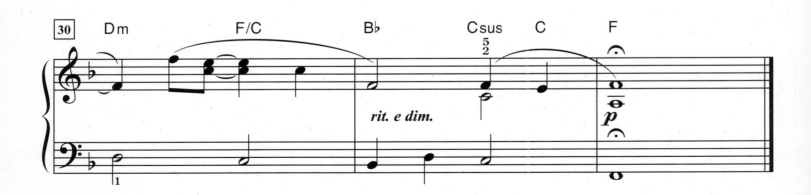

GONNA FLY NOW
(Theme from *Rocky Balboa*)

By Bill Conti, Ayn Robbins and Carol Connors
Arranged by Carol Matz

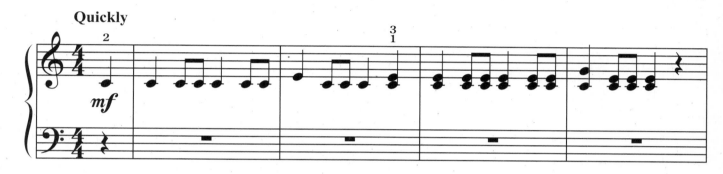

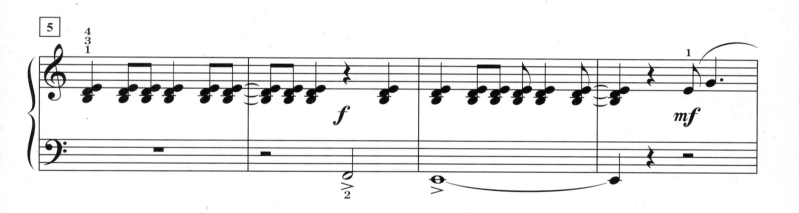

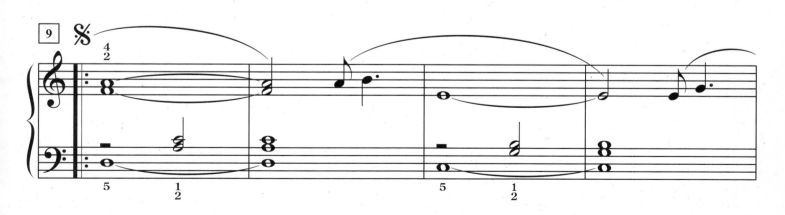

© 1976, 1977 (Copyrights Renewed) UNITED ARTISTS CORPORATION
All Rights Administered by EMI U CATALOG INC./EMI UNART CATALOG INC. (Publishing)
and ALFRED MUSIC PUBLISHING CO., INC. (Print)
All Rights Reserved

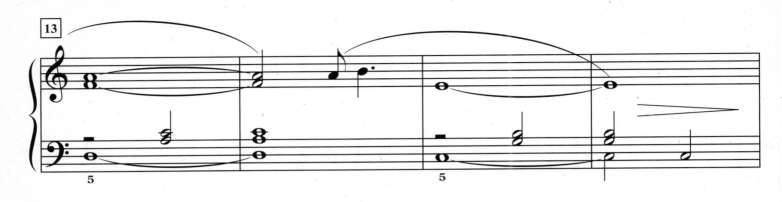

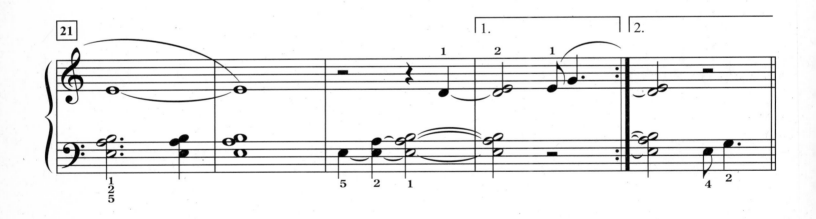

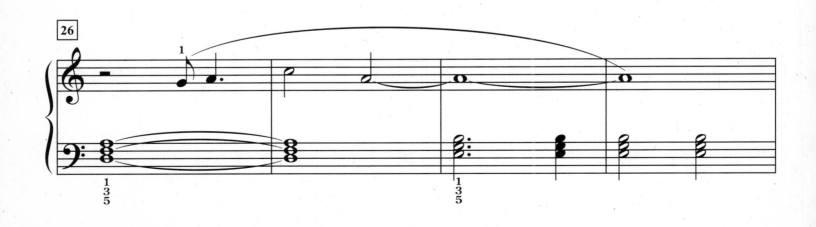

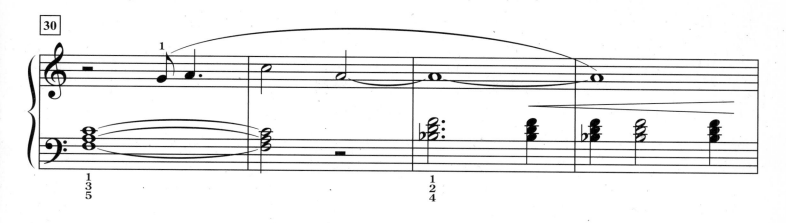

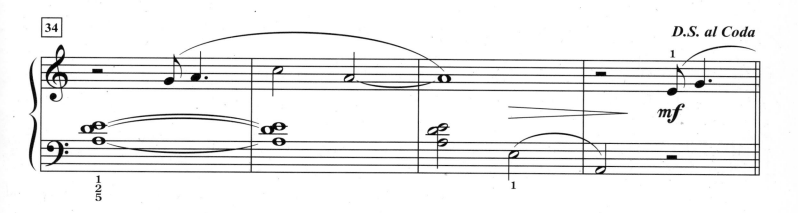

GOTTA BE SOMEBODY

Lyrics by Chad Kroeger
Music by Nickelback
Arranged by Carol Matz

© 2008 WARNER-TAMERLANE PUBLISHING CORP., ARM YOUR DILLO PUBLISHING INC., BLACK DIESEL MUSIC, INC.,
ZERO G MUSIC INC. and BLACK ADDER MUSIC
All Rights Administered by WARNER-TAMERLANE PUBLISHING CORP.
All Rights Reserved

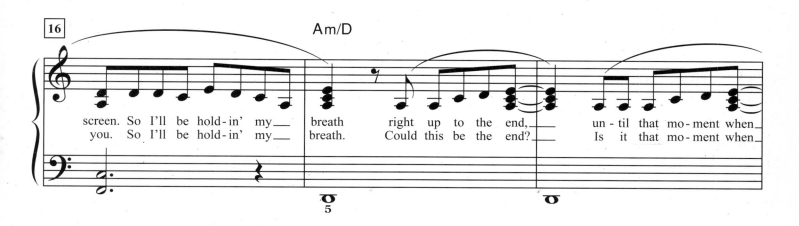

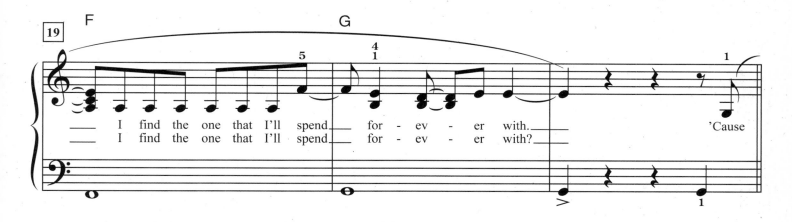

some - one cares. Some-one to love___ with my life in their hands. There's

got - ta be some - bod - y for me like that. 'Cause no - bod - y wants___ to go it

on their own. And ev - 'ry - one wants___ to know they're not a - lone.

Some-bod - y else___ that feels the same some - where. There's got - ta be some - bod - y for

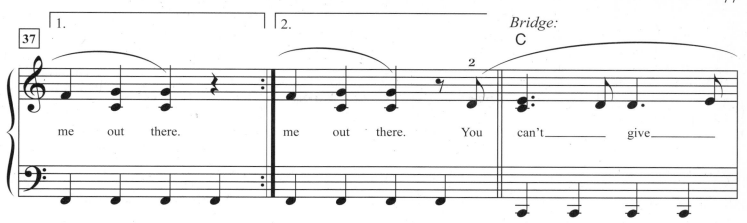

me out there. me out there. You can't_____ give_____

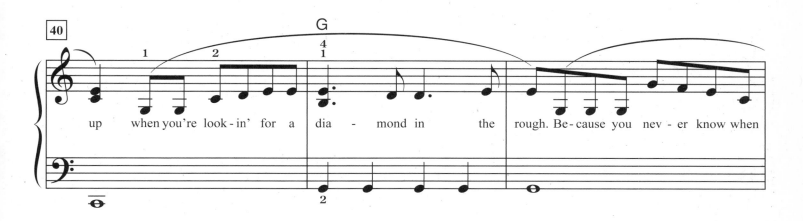

up when you're look-in' for a dia - mond in the rough. Be-cause you nev - er know when

it_____ shows_____ up, make sure you're hold - in on. 'Cause it could be the one,

D.S. al Coda   Coda

the one you're wait-ing on. 'Cause

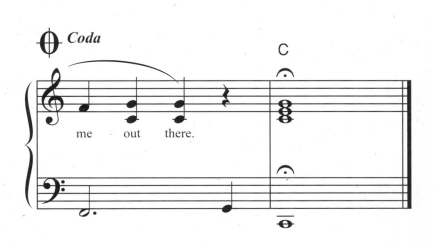

me out there.

HARRY'S WONDROUS WORLD

(from *Harry Potter and The Sorcerer's Stone*)

Music by JOHN WILLIAMS
Arranged by Carol Matz

© 2001 WARNER-BARHAM MUSIC, LLC (BMI)
All Rights Administered by WARNER-TAMERLANE PUBLISHING CORP. (BMI)
All Rights Reserved

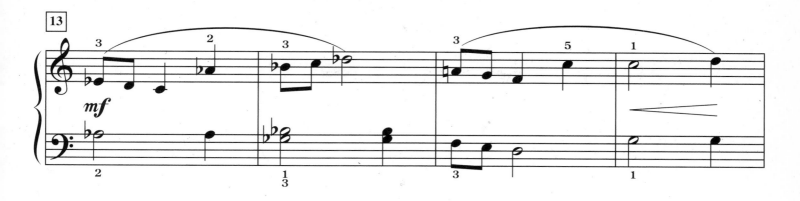

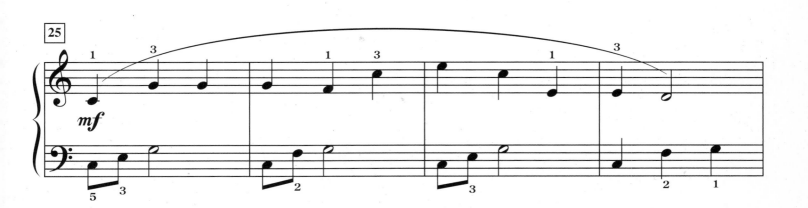

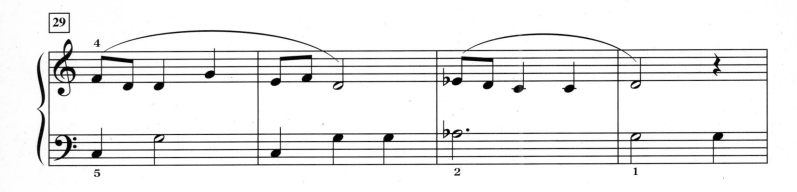

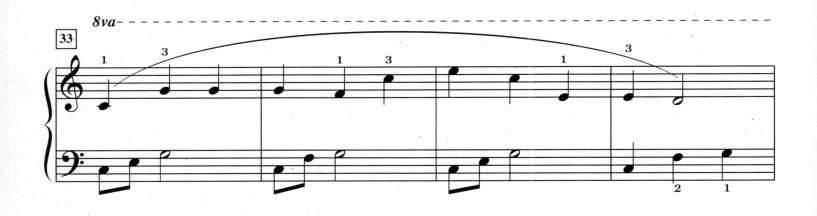

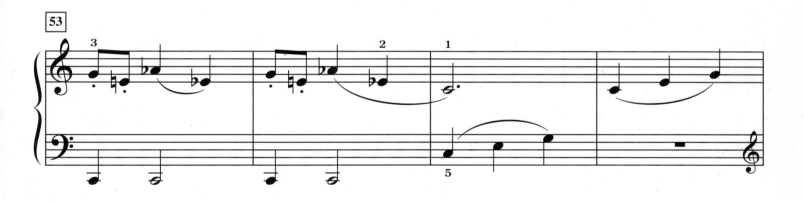

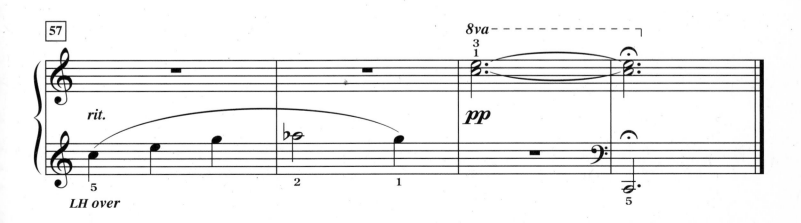

THE HARSHEST PLACE ON EARTH

(from *The March of the Penguins*)

By Alex Wurman
Arranged by Carol Matz

© 2005 WARNER-BARHAM MUSIC LLC (BMI) and SONART PRODUCTIONS (BMI)
All Rights Administered by SONGS OF UNIVERSAL, INC. (BMI)
Exclusive Worldwide Print Rights Administered by ALFRED MUSIC PUBLISHING CO., INC.
All Rights Reserved

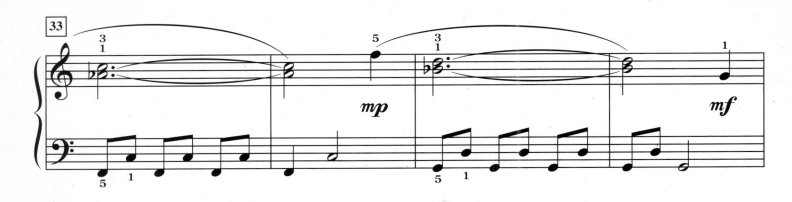

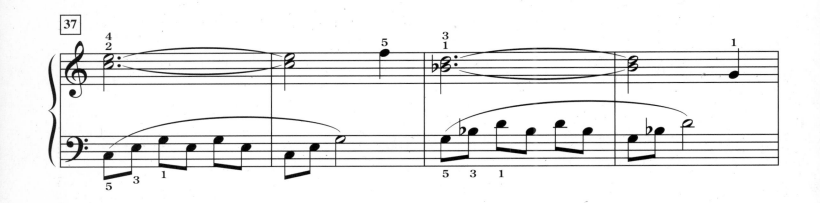

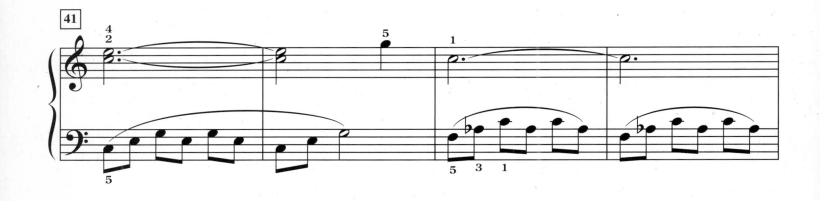

HAVEN'T MET YOU YET

Words and Music by
Michael Bublé, Alan Chang and Amy Foster
Arranged by Carol Matz

© 2009 WB MUSIC CORP., I'M THE LAST MAN STANDING MUSIC, INC., WARNER-TAMERLANE PUBLISHING CORP., IHAN ZHAN
MUSIC and MS. DOE MUSIC
All Rights on behalf of itself and I'M THE LAST MAN STANDING MUSIC, INC. Administered by WB MUSIC CORP.
All Rights on behalf of itself, IHAN ZHAN MUSIC and MS. DOE MUSIC Administered by WARNER-TAMERLANE PUBLISHING CORP.
All Rights Reserved

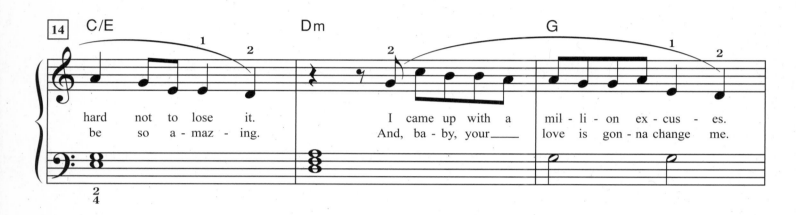

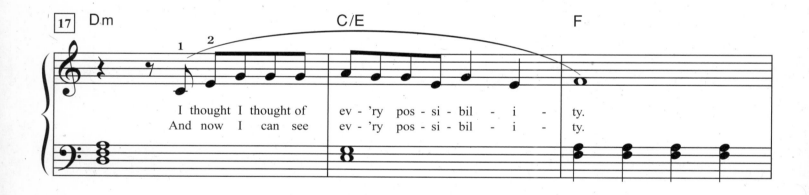

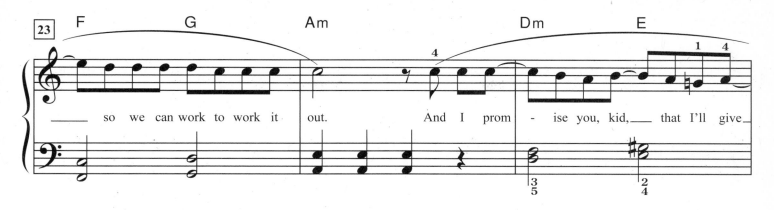

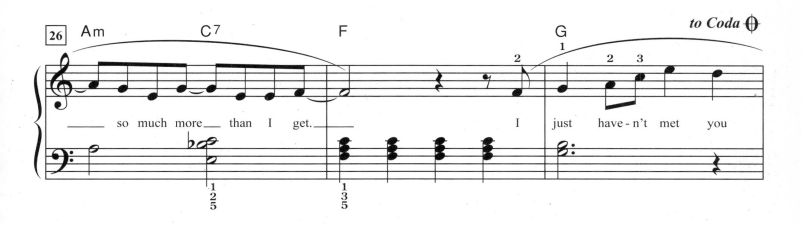

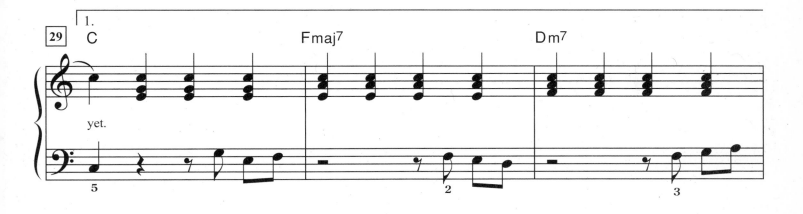

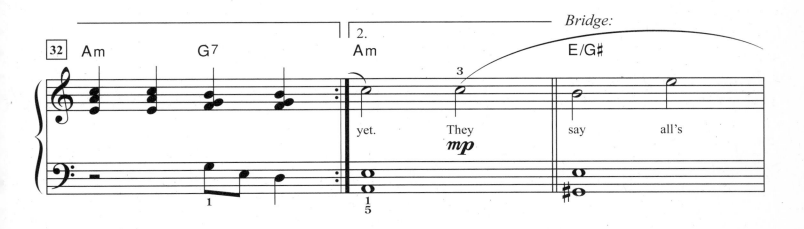

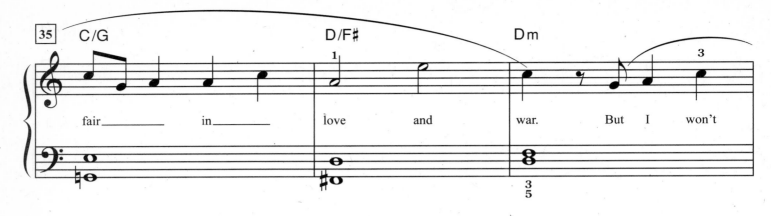

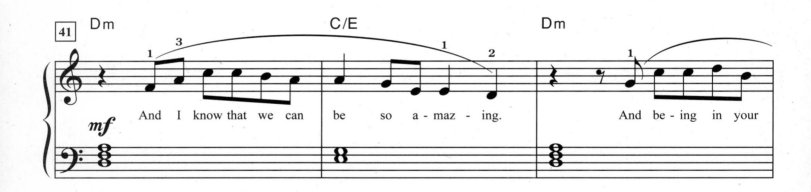

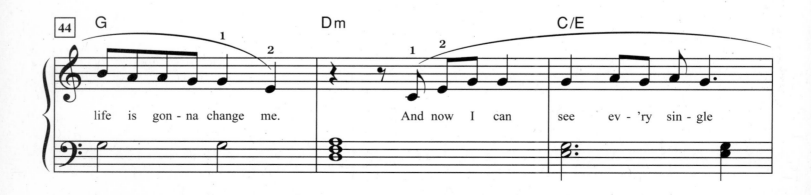

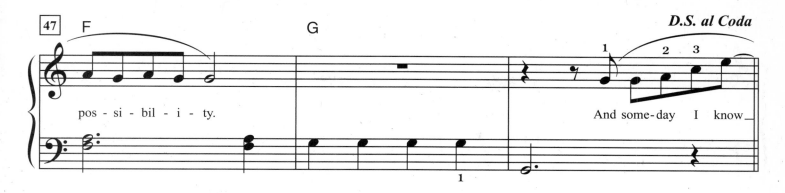

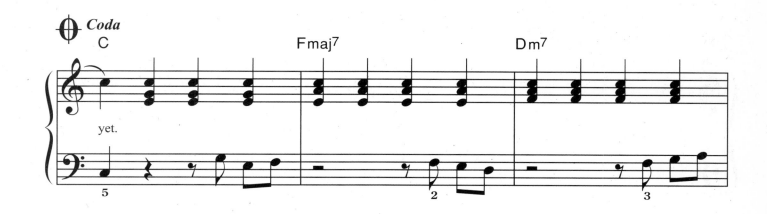

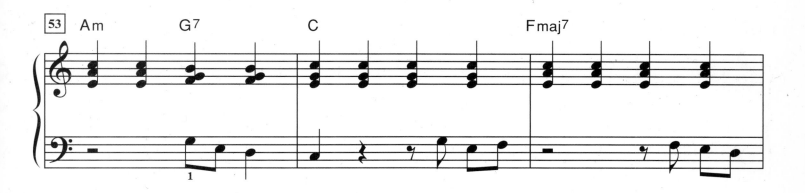

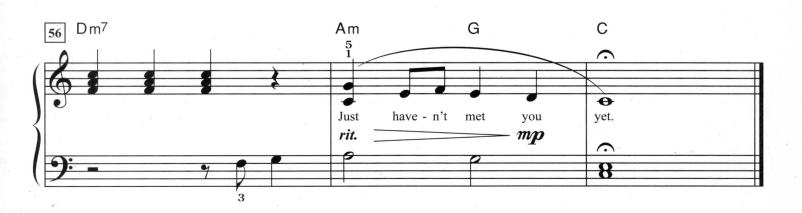

HEDWIG'S THEME

(from *Harry Potter and The Sorcerer's Stone*)

Music by JOHN WILLIAMS
Arranged by Carol Matz

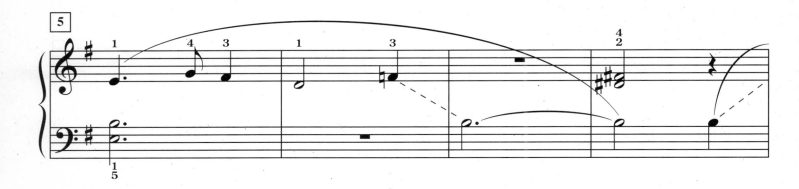

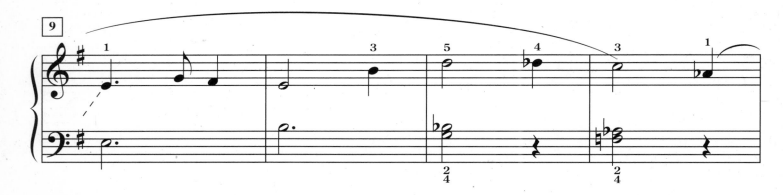

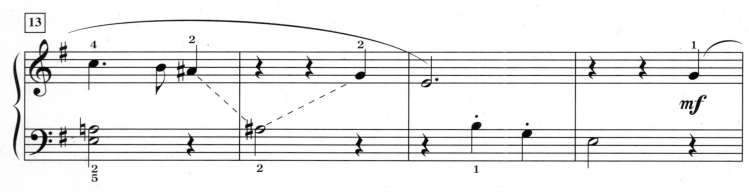

© 2002 WARNER-BARHAM MUSIC LLC (BMI)
All Rights Administered by SONGS OF UNIVERSAL (BMI)
Exclusive Worldwide Print Rights Administered by ALFRED MUSIC PUBLISHING CO., INC.
All Rights Reserved

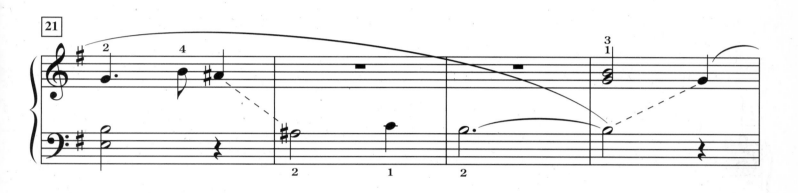

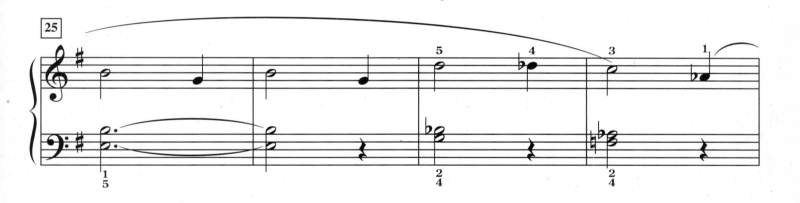

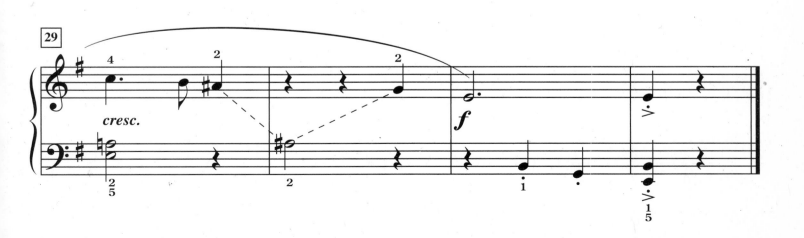

HEY THERE DELILAH

Moderately

Verse:

Words and Music by Tom Higgenson
Arranged by Carol Matz

© 2005 WB MUSIC CORP., FEARMORE MUSIC and SO HAPPY PUBLISHING
All Rights Administered by WB MUSIC CORP.
All Rights Reserved

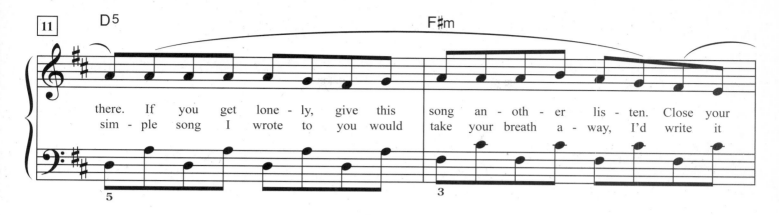

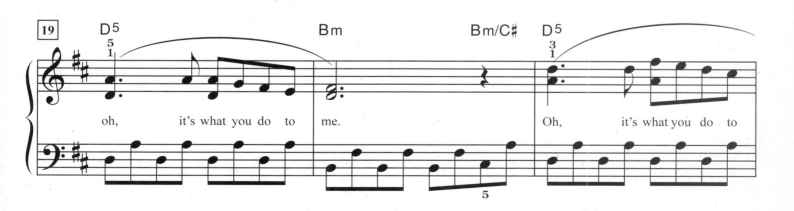

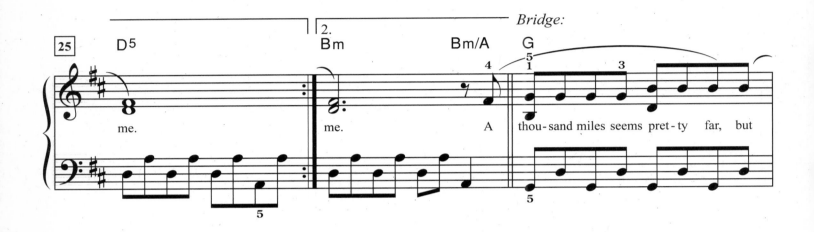

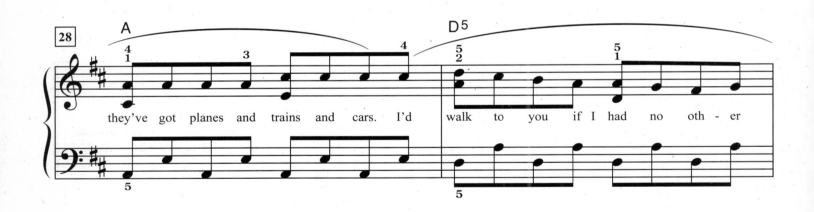

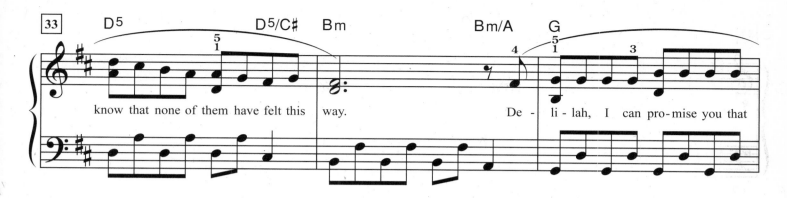

know that none of them have felt this way. De - li - lah, I can pro-mise you that

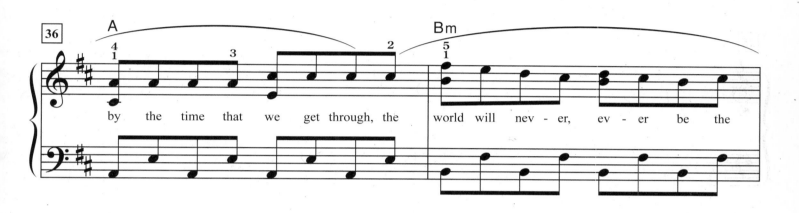

by the time that we get through, the world will nev - er, ev - er be the

D.S. al Coda

same, and you're to blame.

Coda

me. What you do to me.

HOT N COLD

Words and Music by
Katy Perry, Lukasz Gottwald and Max Martin
Arranged by Carol Matz

© 2008 WHEN I'M RICH YOU'LL BE MY BITCH, KASZ MONEY PUBLISHING and UNIVERSAL MUSIC-MGB SONGS
All Rights for WHEN I'M RICH YOU'LL BE MY BITCH Administered by WB MUSIC CORP.
All Rights Reserved

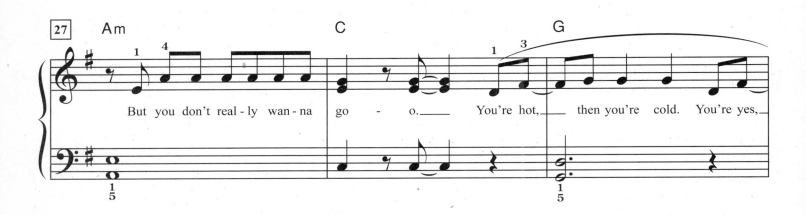

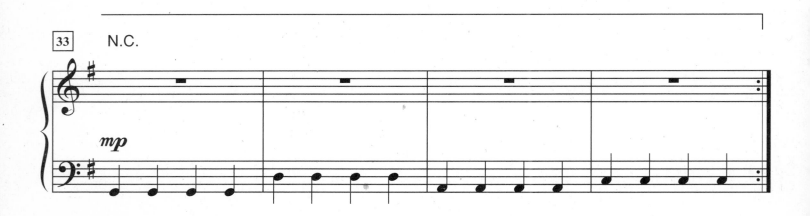

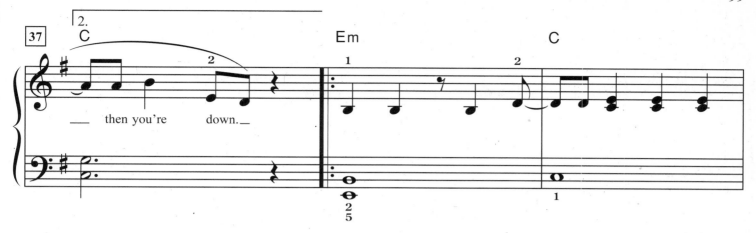

Bridge:

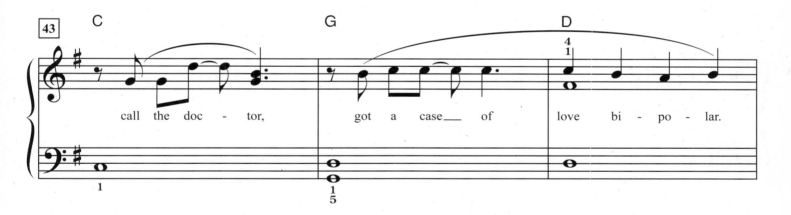

ride._____ You change your mind

p

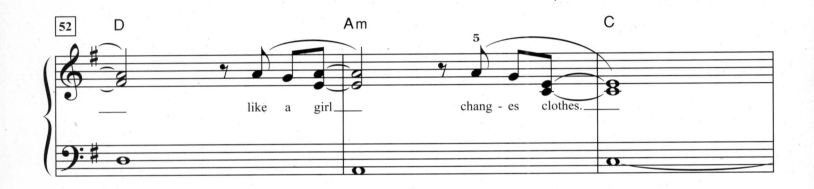

like a girl_____ chang - es clothes._____

D.S. al Coda   **Coda**

'Cause you're hot,

mf

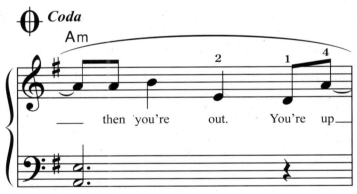

_____ then you're out. You're up_____

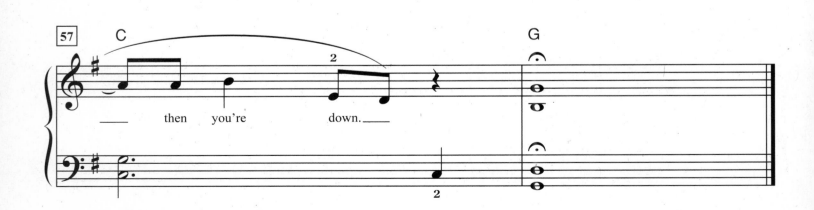

_____ then you're down._____

I DIDN'T KNOW MY OWN STRENGTH

Words and Music by Diane Warren
Arranged by Carol Matz

© 2009 REALSONGS (ASCAP)
All Rights Reserved

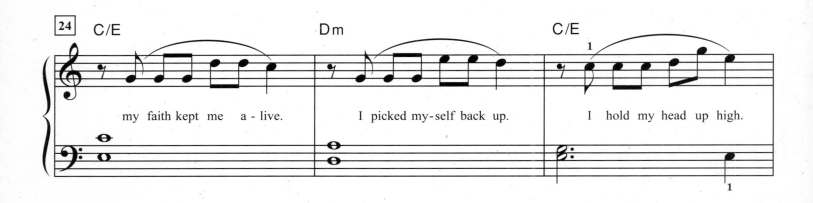

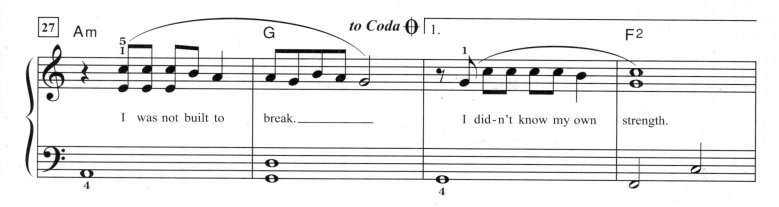

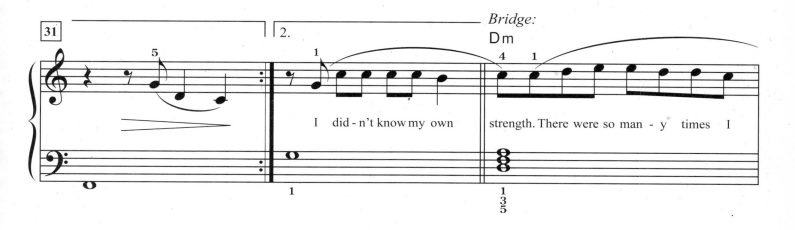

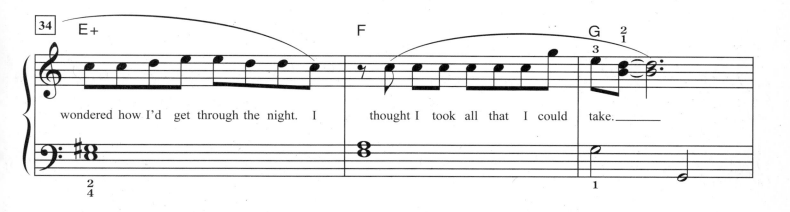

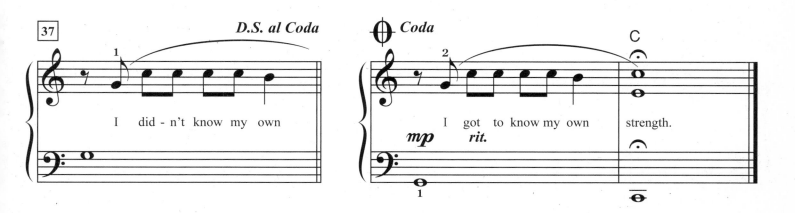

I KISSED A GIRL

Words and Music by
Katy Perry, Lukasz Gottwald,
Max Martin and Cathy Dennis
Arranged by Carol Matz

© 2008 WHEN I'M RICH YOU'LL BE MY BITCH, KASZ MONEY PUBLISHING, UNIVERSAL MUSIC-MGB SONGS
and EMI MUSIC PUBLISHING LTD
All Rights for WHEN I'M RICH YOU'LL BE MY BITCH Administered by WB MUSIC CORP.
All Rights Reserved

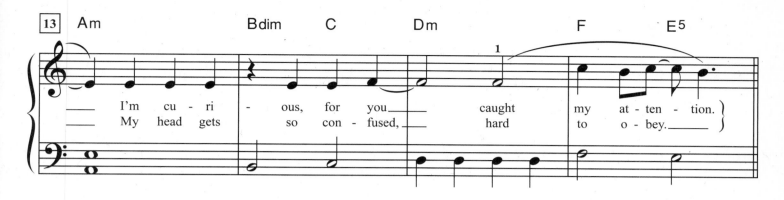

13 | Am | Bdim C | Dm | F E5

I'm cu-ri - ous, for you___ caught my at-ten - tion.
My head gets so con-fused, hard to o-bey.___

℅ *Chorus:*

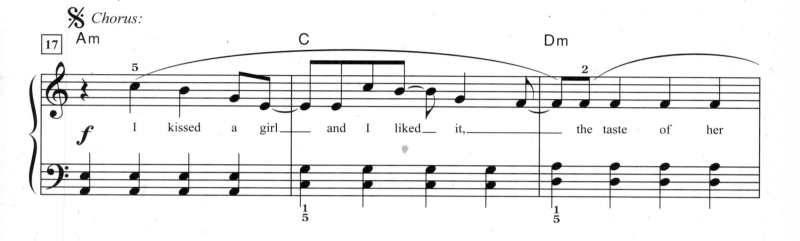

17 | Am | C | Dm

f
I kissed a girl___ and I liked___ it,___ the taste of her

20 | F5 E5 | Am | C

cher-ry chap-stick. I kissed a girl___ just to try___ it.___

23 | Dm | F5 E5 | Am

I hope my boy - friend don't mind___ it. It felt so wrong,___

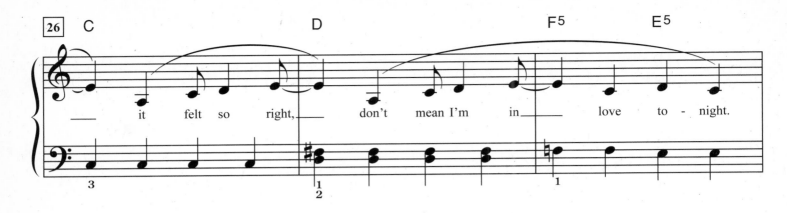

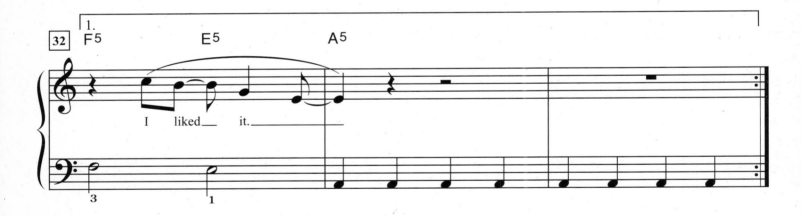

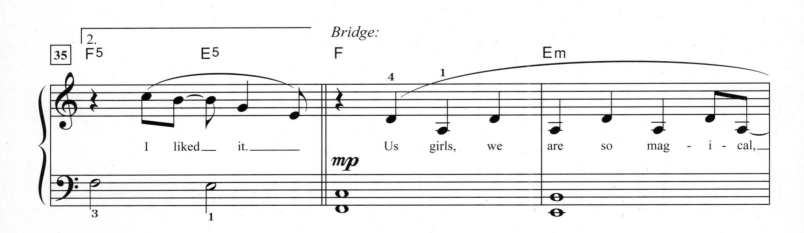

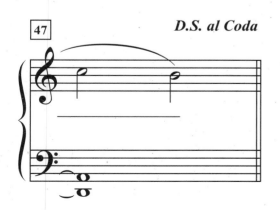

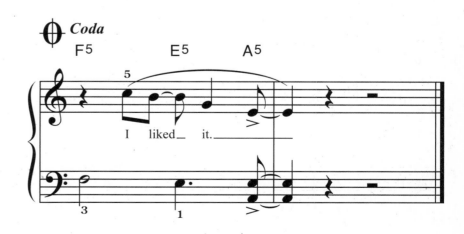

I'LL KEEP YOUR MEMORY VAGUE

Music and Lyrics by Scott Anderson, Sean Anderson,
Rich Beddoe, James Black and Rick Jackett
Arranged by Carol Matz

© 2007 FSMGI (IMRO) and FINGER ELEVEN PUBLISHING (SOCAN)
All Rights Administered by STATE ONE SONGS AMERICA (ASCAP)
All Rights Reserved

Chorus:

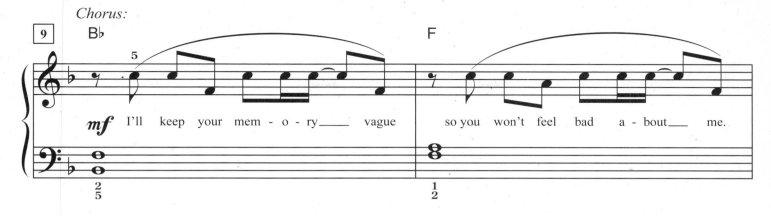

9 Bb   F

mf I'll keep your mem - o - ry___ vague   so you won't feel bad a - bout___ me.

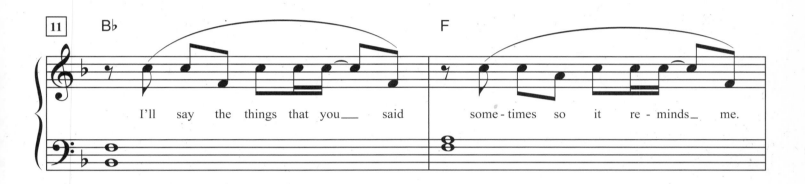

11 Bb   F

I'll say the things that you___ said   some - times so it re - minds___ me.

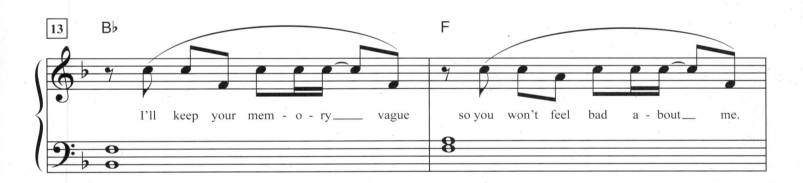

13 Bb   F

I'll keep your mem - o - ry___ vague   so you won't feel bad a - bout___ me.

15 C   Bb

I'll say the things that you said   some - times so it re - minds___ me.   *mp*

Verse:

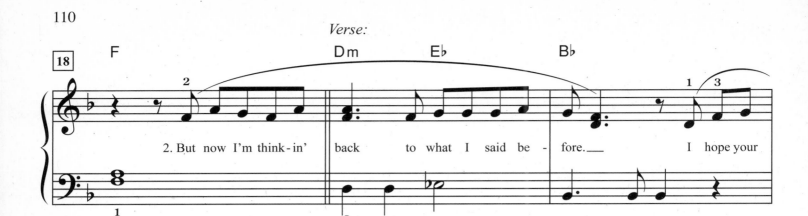

2. But now I'm think-in' back to what I said be - fore.___ I hope your

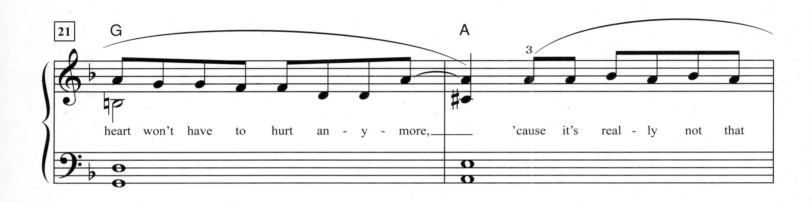

heart won't have to hurt an - y - more,___ 'cause it's real - ly not that

sad___ from here,___ be - cause the mo - ments I can feel you near,

___ they keep you close to me, my dear, and if they ev - er be-come too clear...___

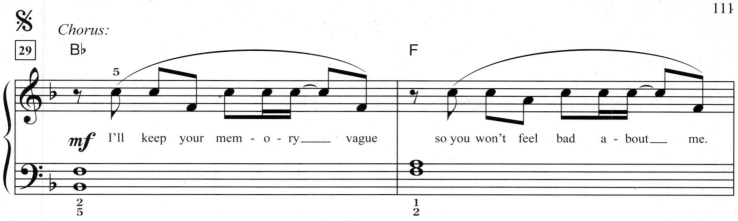

Chorus:

29 B♭ / F

mf I'll keep your mem - o - ry____ vague / so you won't feel bad a - bout____ me.

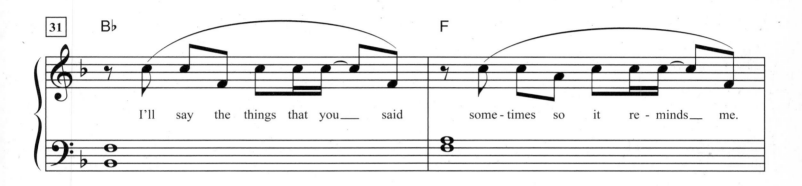

31 B♭ / F

I'll say the things that you____ said / some - times so it re - minds____ me.

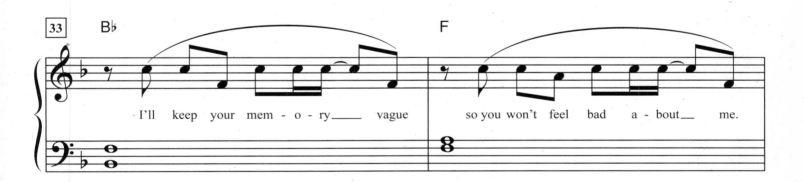

33 B♭ / F

I'll keep your mem - o - ry____ vague / so you won't feel bad a - bout____ me.

35 C / *to Coda*

I'll say the things that you said / some - times so it re - minds____ me.

Bridge:

Now you're gone___ a - way. Don't wor - ry it's o - kay that you're gone___ a - way.

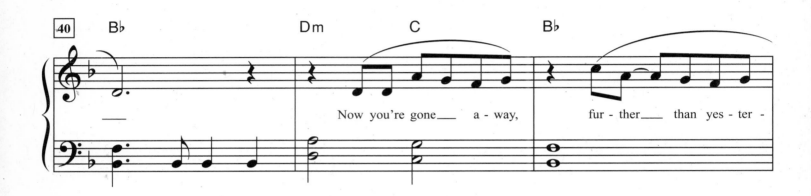

___ Now you're gone___ a - way, fur - ther___ than yes - ter -

D.S. al Coda

day, but you nev - er leave___ these scenes___ my mind___ re - plays.___

Coda

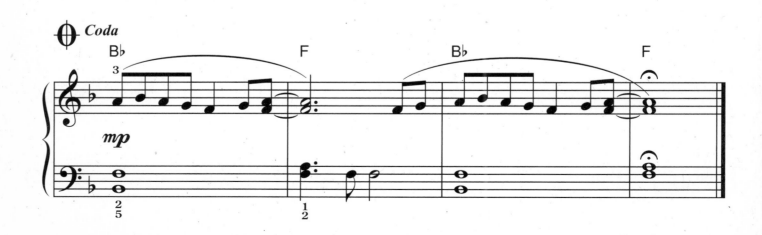

INSIDE YOUR HEAVEN

Words and Music by
Andreas Carlsson, Per Nylen and Savan Kotecha
Arranged by Carol Matz

© 2005 WB MUSIC CORP., ANDREAS CARLSSON PUBLISHING AB, UNIVERSAL MUSIC PUBLISHING AB and OH SUKI MUSIC
All Rights on behalf of itself and ANDREAS CARLSSON PUBLISHING AB Administered by WB MUSIC CORP. All Rights Reserved

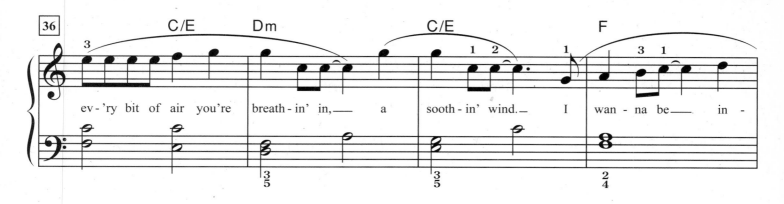

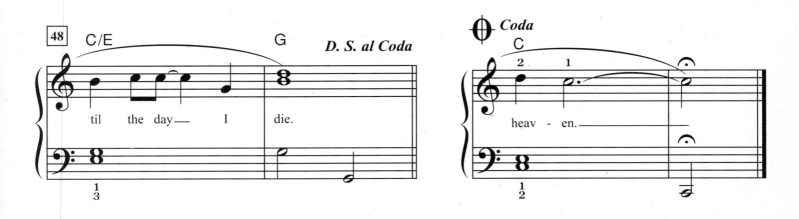

IN MY ARMS

Words and Music by Tiffany Lee Arbuckle,
Matt Bronleewe and Jeremy Bose
Arranged by Carol Matz

© 2007 SHOECRAZY PUBLISHING (SESAC) (Administered by CURB CONGREGATION SONGS),
WOODLAND CREATURES NEED MUSIC TOO (ASCAP), MUSIC OF WINDSWEPT (ASCAP)
MEADOWGREEN MUSIC COMPANY (ASCAP) and VANDELAY PUBLISHING (ASCAP)
All Rights on behalf of itself and WOODLAND CREATURES NEED MUSIC TOO Administered by MUSIC OF WINDSWEPT
All Rights For MEADOWGREEN MUSIC COMPANY and VANDELAY PUBLISHING Administered by EMI CMG PUBLISHING
All Rights Reserved   Used by Permission

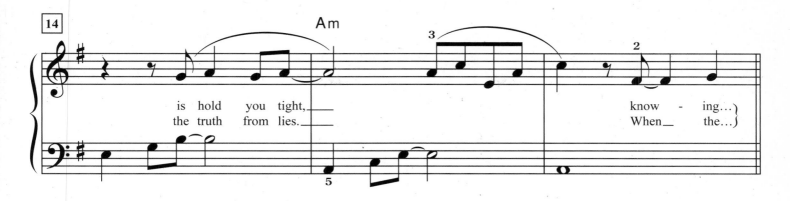

is hold you tight, ___ knowing...)
the truth from lies. ___ When ___ the...)

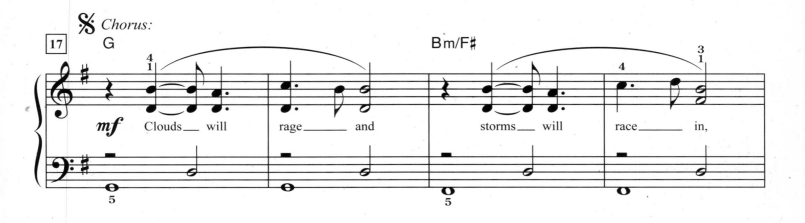

% *Chorus:*

mf Clouds ___ will rage ___ and storms ___ will race ___ in,

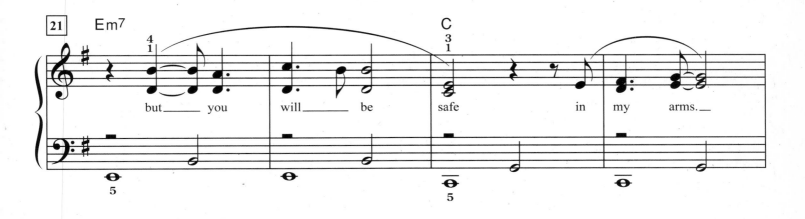

but ___ you will ___ be safe in my arms. ___

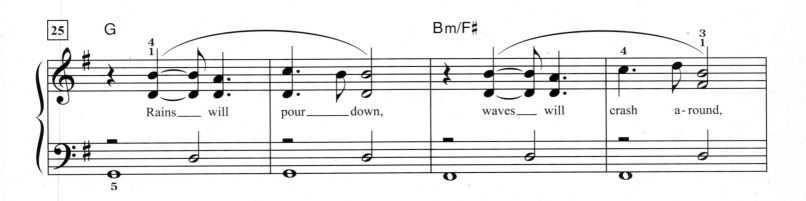

Rains ___ will pour ___ down, waves ___ will crash a-round,

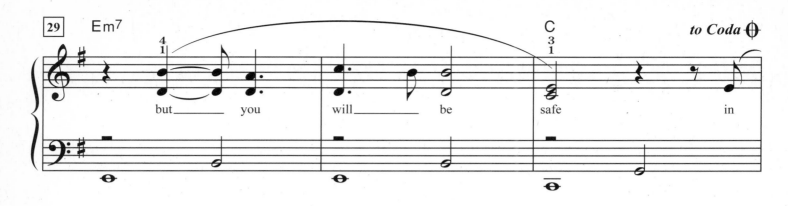

but_____ you will_____ be safe in

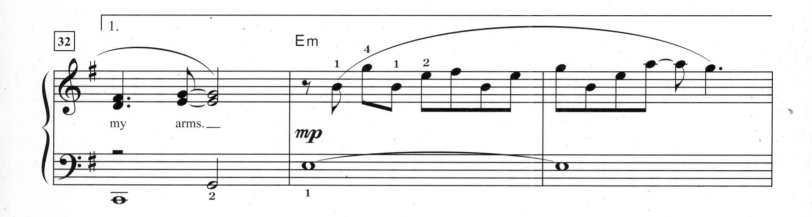

my arms.___

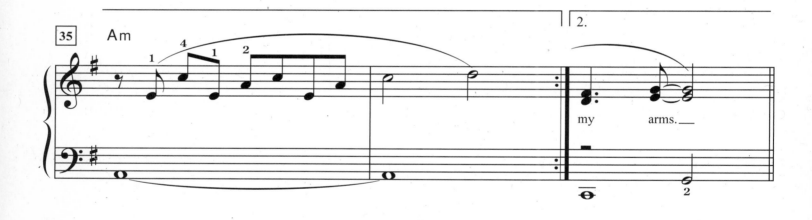

my arms.___

Bridge:

Cas - tles, they__ may crum - ble._____

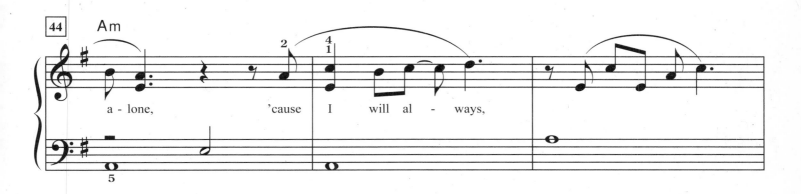

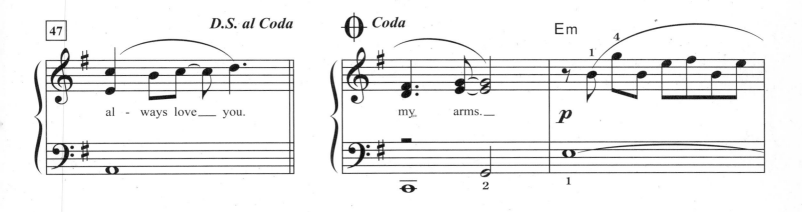

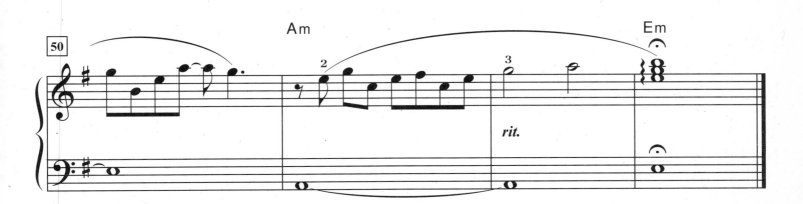

JAMES BOND THEME

By Monty Norman
Arranged by Carol Matz

Quickly, mysteriously

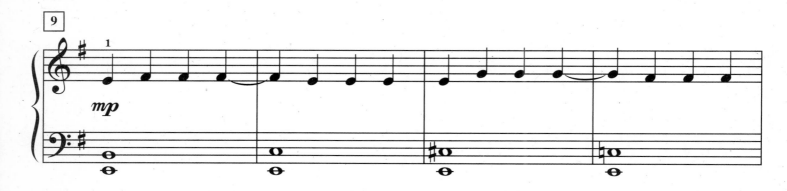

© 1962 UNITED ARTISTS MUSIC LTD.
Copyright Renewed by EMI UNART CATALOG, INC.
Exclusive Print Rights Administered by ALFRED MUSIC PUBLISHING CO., INC.
All Rights Reserved

INTO THE WEST

(from *The Lord of the Rings: The Return of the King*)

Words and Music by
Howard Shore, Fran Walsh and Annie Lennox
Arranged by Carol Matz

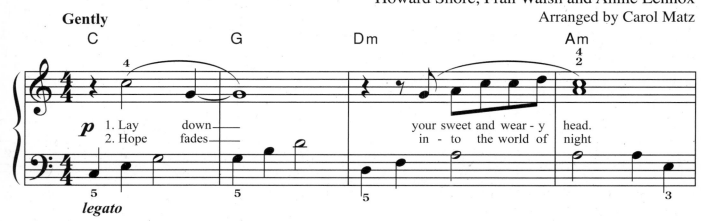

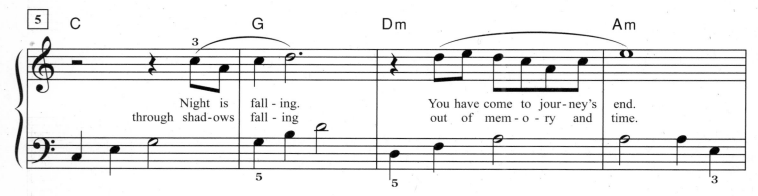

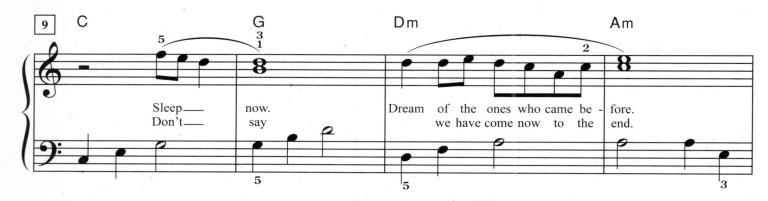

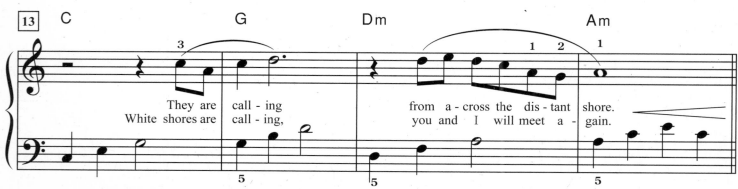

© 2003 NEW LINE TUNES (ASCAP), SOUTH FIFTH AVENUE PUBLISHING (ASCAP) and LA LENNOXA LTD.
All Rights for NEW LINE TUNES (ASCAP) Administered by UNIVERSAL MUSIC CORPORATION (ASCAP)
All Rights for LA LENNOXA LTD. Administered by UNIVERSAL–MGB SONGS
Exclusive Worldwide Print Rights for NEW LINE TUNES (ASCAP) and SOUTH FIFTH AVENUE PUBLISHING (ASCAP) Administered by
ALFRED MUSIC PUBLISHING CO., INC.
All Rights Reserved

LOVE WILL ALWAYS WIN

Words and Music by
Wayne Kirkpatrick and Gordon Kennedy
Arranged by Carol Matz

Moderately
Verse:

Hold on like there's no to-mor-row, there can be no

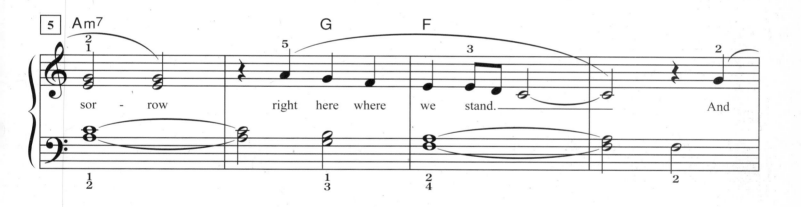

sor-row right here where we stand. And

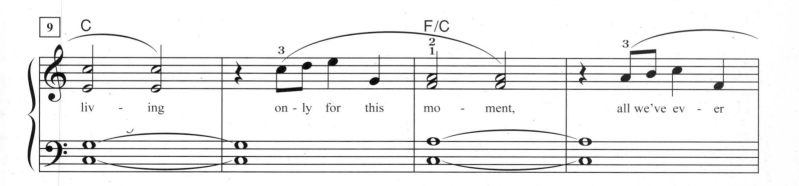

liv-ing on-ly for this mo-ment, all we've ev-er

© 1999 WARNER-TAMERLANE PUBLISHING CORP., SELL THE COW MUSIC, UNIVERSAL POLYGRAM INTERNATIONAL
and SONDANCE KID MUSIC.
All Rights on behalf of itself and SELL THE COW MUSIC Administered by WARNER-TAMERLANE PUBLISHING CORP.
All Rights Reserved

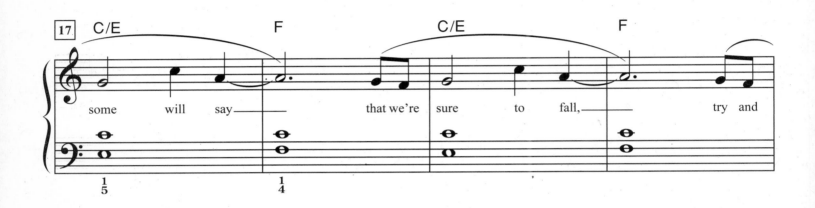

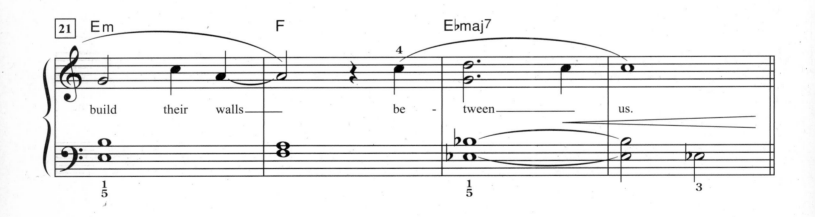

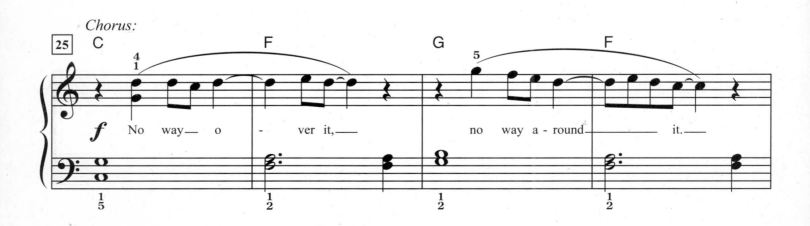

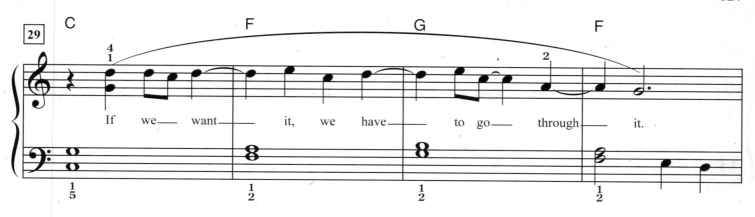

If we want it, we have to go through it.

Fight for love and the world tries to break us down.

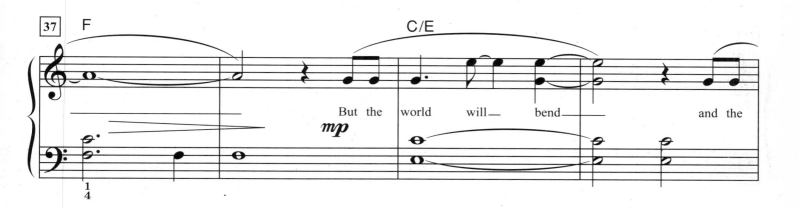

But the world will bend and the

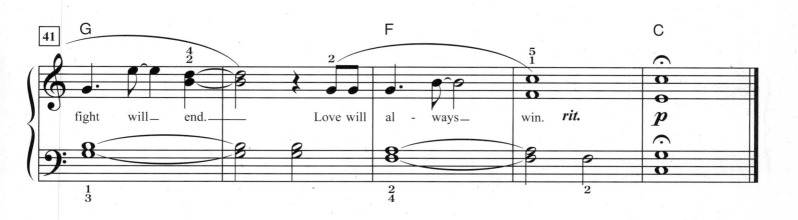

fight will end. Love will al - ways win.

KNOW YOUR ENEMY

Lyrics by Billie Joe
Music by Green Day
Arranged by Carol Matz

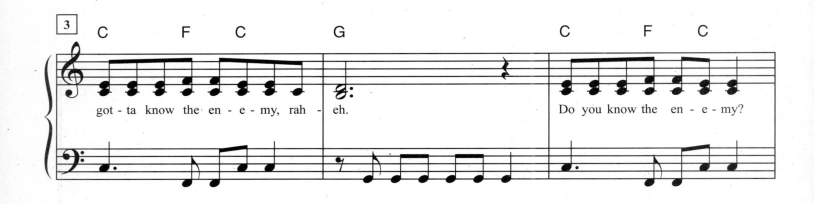

© 2009 WB MUSIC CORP. and GREEN DAZE MUSIC
All Rights Administered by WB MUSIC CORP.
All Rights Reserved

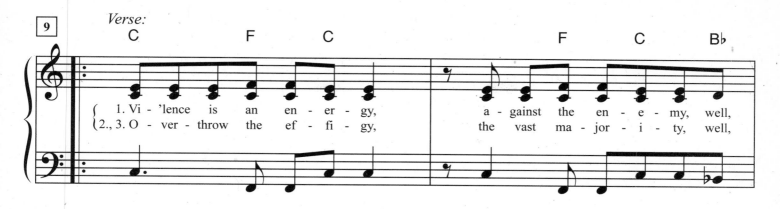

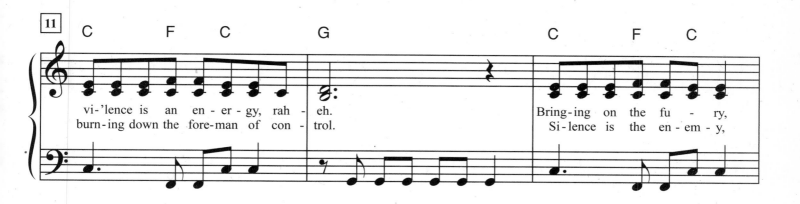

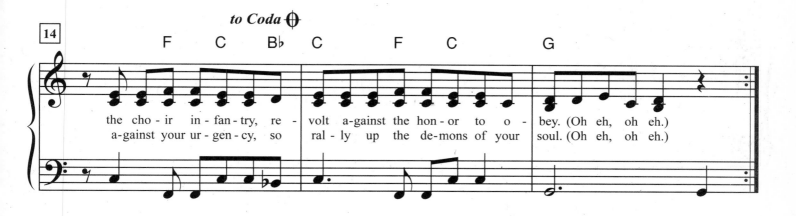

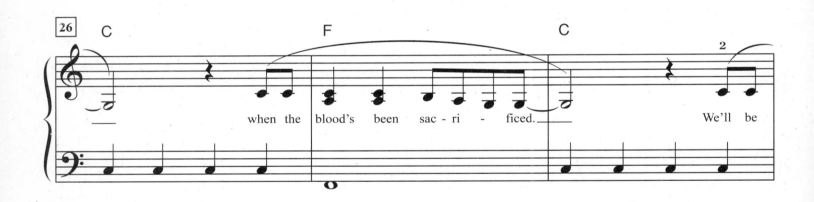

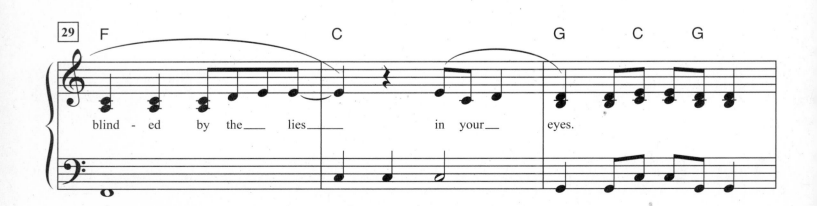

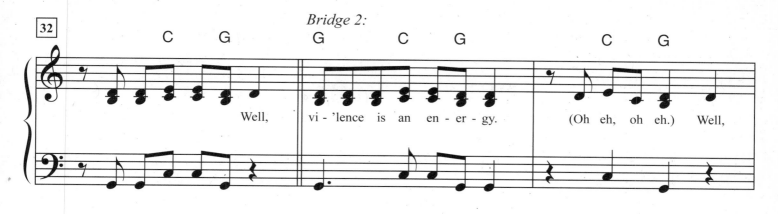

LET IT ROCK

Words and Music by Kevin Rudolf and Dwayne Carter
Arranged by Carol Matz

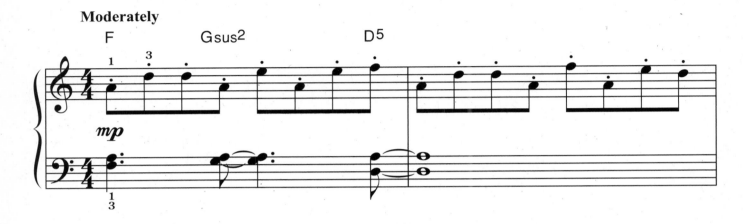

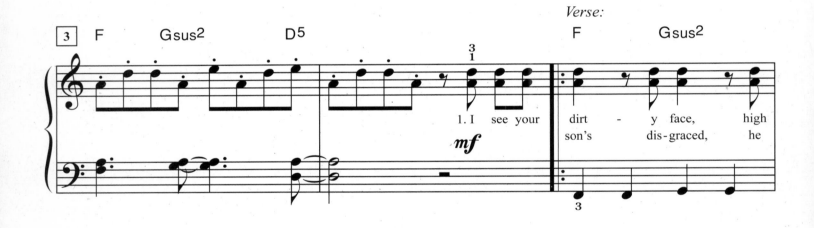

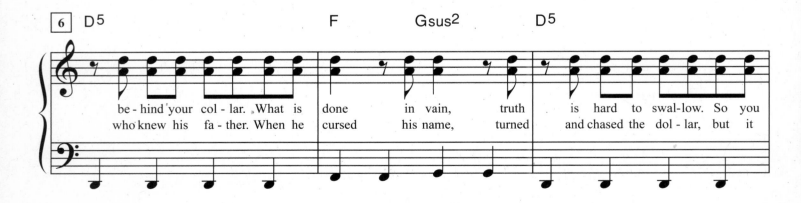

© 2008 WARNER-TAMERLANE PUBLISHING CORP., LION AIRE PUBLISHING and YOUNG MONEY PUBLISHING, INC. All Rights Administered by WARNER-TAMERLANE PUBLISHING CORP.
All Rights Reserved

Chorus:

I ar - rive, I, I'll bring the fi - re. Make you come a - live, I

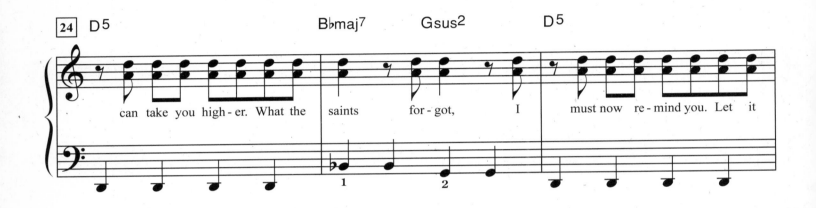

can take you high - er. What the saints for - got, I must now re - mind you. Let it

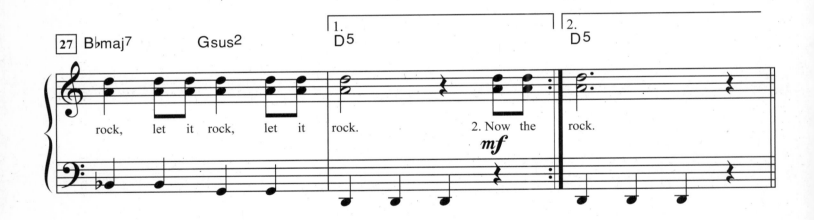

rock, let it rock, let it rock. 2. Now the rock.

LOVE IS FREE

Words and Music by Sheryl Crow and Bill Bottrell
Arranged by Carol Matz

© 2008 FSMGI (IMRO) and IGNORANT MUSIC
All Rights for FSMGI (IMRO) Administered by STATE ONE SONGS AMERICA (ASCAP)
All Rights Reserved

We go to town, no one's a - round, 'cause if you drown,

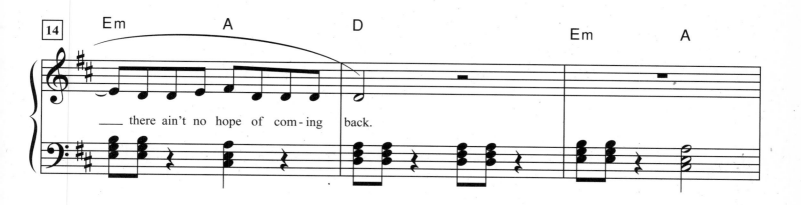

____ there ain't no hope of com - ing back.

It ain't no big thing if you lose your faith.____ They kind - a like to keep you

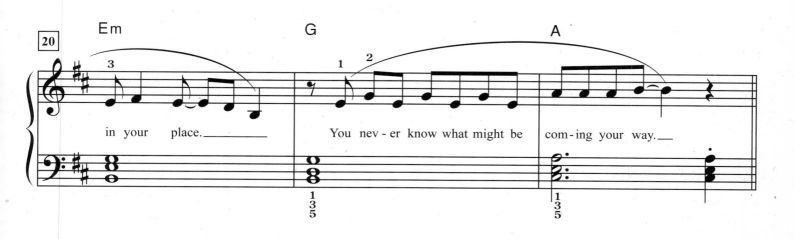

in your place.____ You nev - er know what might be com - ing your way.____

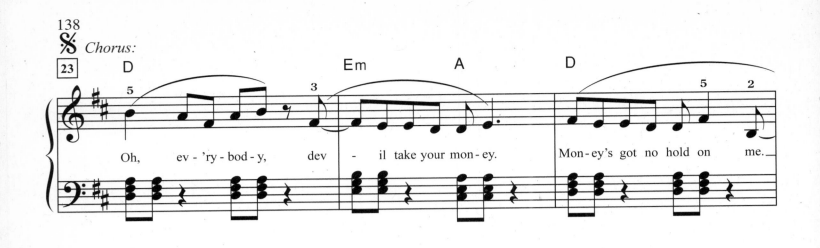

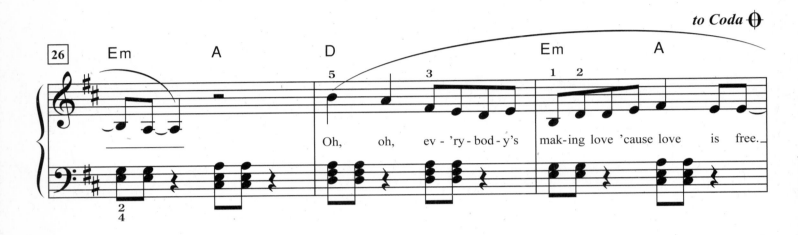

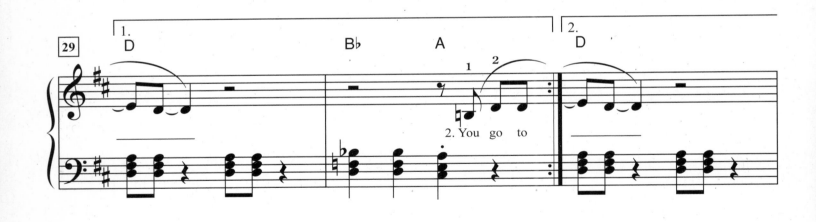

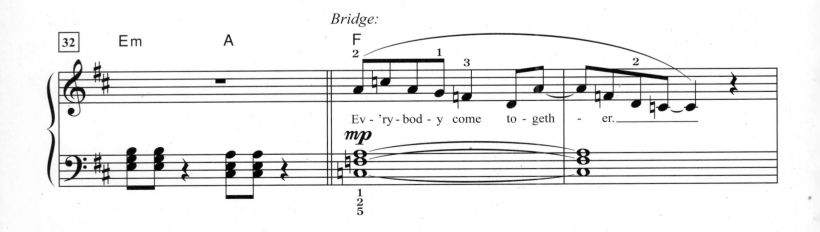

Verse 2:
You go to church and pray to God for no more rain.
Cadillac, paper sack, well, hey there, Jack,
you want some bourbon for the pain?
Hey, tambourine, ain't no rhythm on the street.
With the voodoo, what do you do
when the radio just plays on anyway?
Those greasy fingers in your jelly jar,
they'll jack your money while you sleep in your car.
They got the karma, they ain't gettin' too far.

MY LIFE WOULD SUCK WITHOUT YOU

Words and Music by
Claude Kelly, Lukasz Gottwald and Max Martin
Arranged by Carol Matz

© 2008 WARNER-TAMERLANE PUBLISHING CORP., STUDIO BEAST MUSIC, KASZ MONEY PUBLISHING
and KOBALT SONGS MUSIC PUBLISHING
All Rights on behalf of itself and STUDIO BEAST MUSIC Administered by WARNER-TAMERLANE PUBLISHING CORP.
All Rights Reserved

Said you'd nev - er come back,__ but here you are__ a - gain.

Chorus:

'Cause we be - long__ to - geth -

- er now,__ yeah. For - ev - er u - nit -

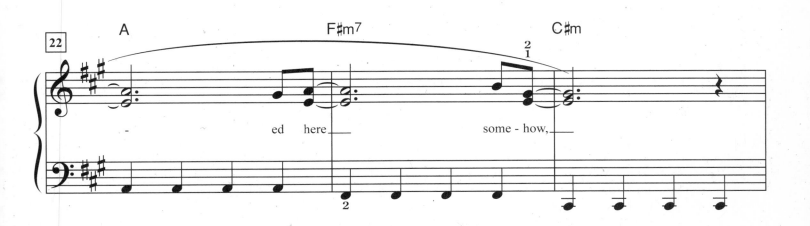

- ed here__ some - how,__

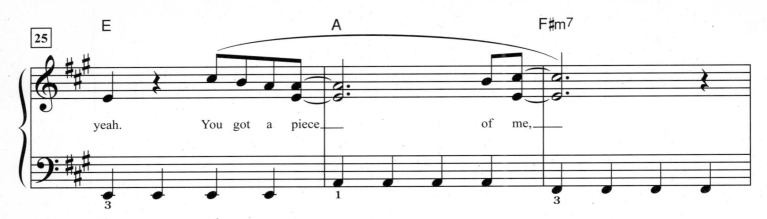

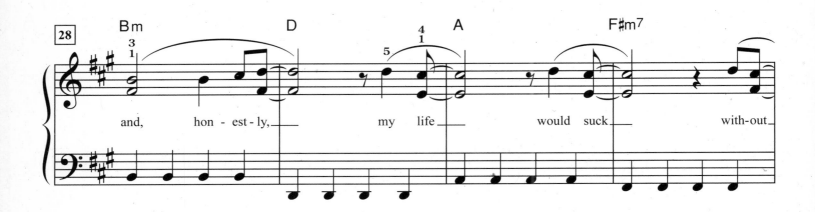

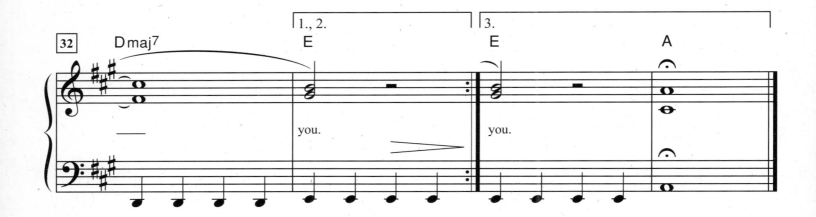

Verse 2:
Baby, I was stupid for telling you goodbye.
Maybe I was wrong for tryin' to pick a fight.
I know that I've got issues, but you're pretty messed up too.
Either way, I found out I'm nothing without you.

Verse 3:
Being with you is so dysfunctional.
I really shouldn't miss you, but I can't let you go, oh, yeah.
(Instrumental)

THE NOTEBOOK

(Main Title)

Written by Aaron Zigman
Arranged by Carol Matz

Slowly, freely

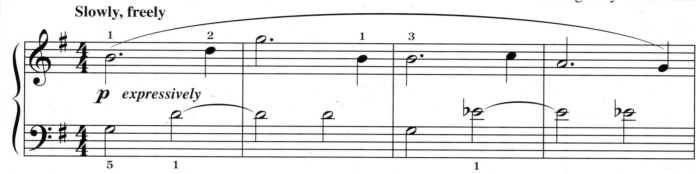

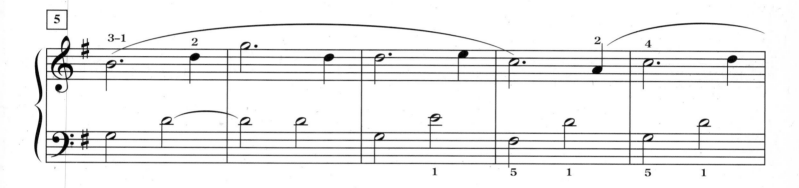

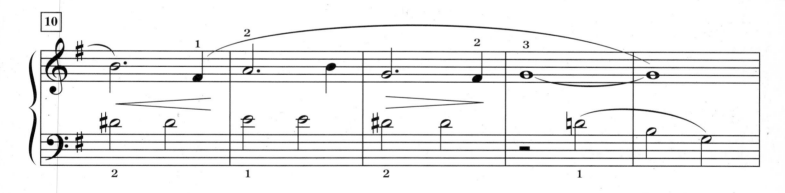

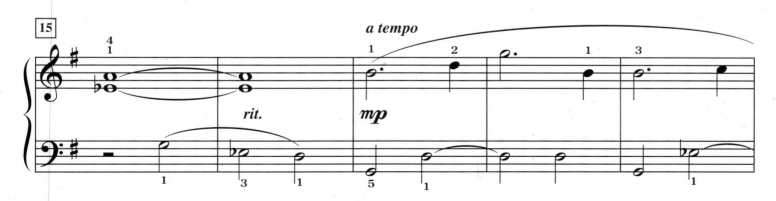

© 2004 NEW LINE MUSIC CORP. (BMI)
All Rights Administered by SONGS OF UNIVERSAL, INC. (BMI)
Exclusive Worldwide Print Rights Administered by ALFRED MUSIC PUBLISHING CO., INC.
All Rights Reserved

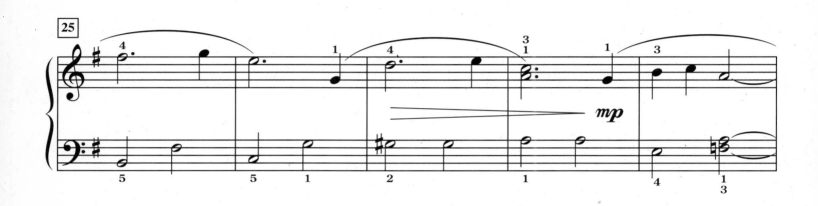

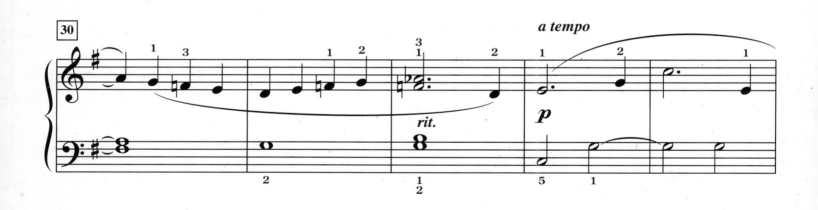

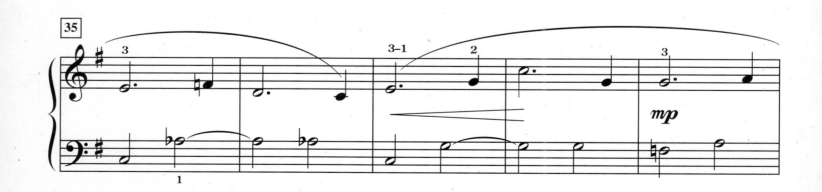

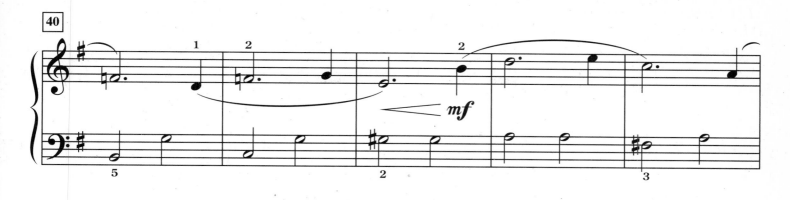

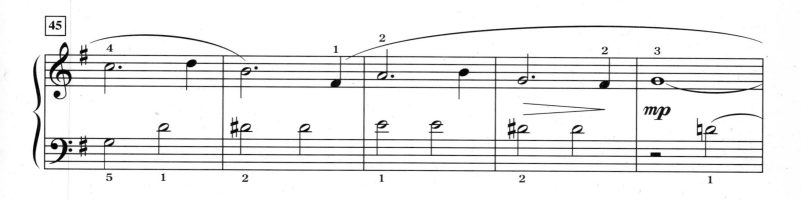

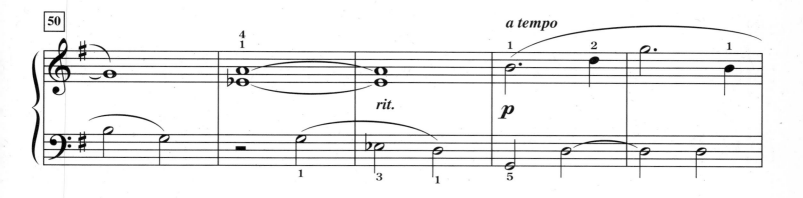

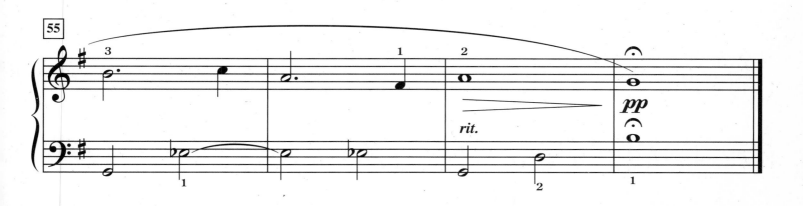

THE NEW GIRL IN TOWN

(from *Hairspray*)

Lyrics by Scott Wittman and Marc Shaiman
Music by Marc Shaiman
Arranged by Carol Matz

© 2007 NEW LINE TUNES (ASCAP) All Rights Administered by UNIVERSAL MUSIC CORP. (ASCAP)
Exclusive Worldwide Print Rights Administered by ALFRED MUSIC PUBLISHING CO., INC.
All Rights Reserved

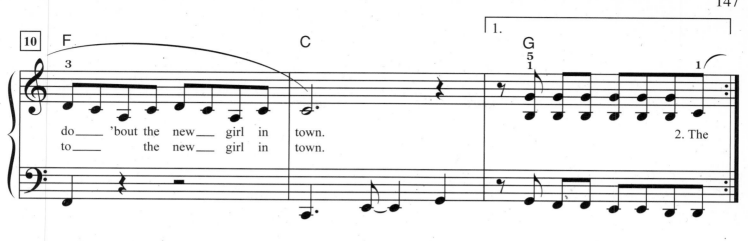

10 F — C — **1.** G

do___ 'bout the new___ girl in town.
to___ the new___ girl in town.

2. The

Bridge:

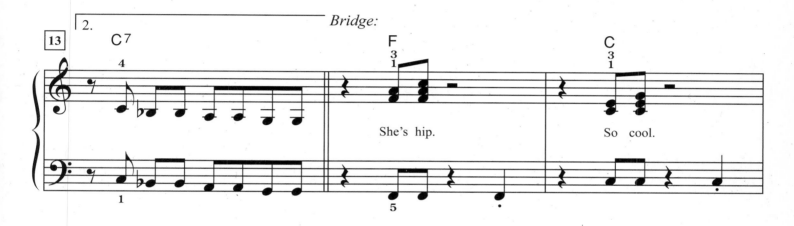

2. **13** C7 — F — C

She's hip.

So cool.

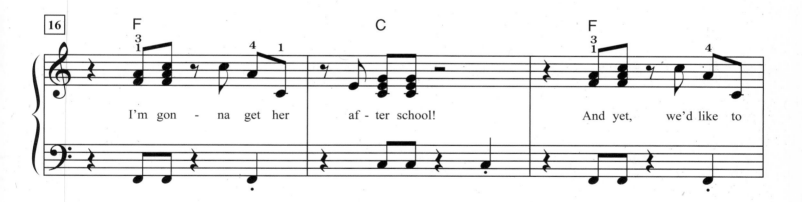

16 F — C — F

I'm gon - na get her   af - ter school!   And yet,   we'd like to

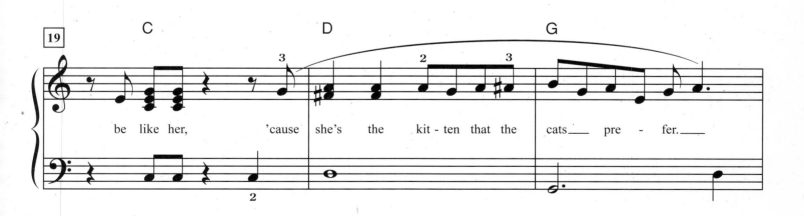

19 C — D — G

be like her,   'cause she's the kit - ten that the   cats___ pre - fer.___

Verse 3:

3. The new girl in town___ has my guy on a string.___ The

new girl in town,___ hey look, she's wear - ing his ring!___

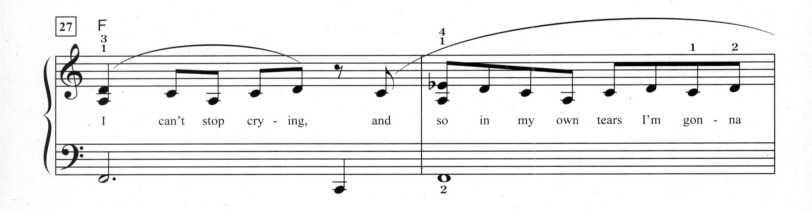

I can't stop cry - ing, and so in my own tears I'm gon - na

drown.___ Whoa,___ whoa,___ whoa,___ whoa, 'cause he wants to ren - dez -

vous__ with the new__ girl. We're kind-a sad and blue.__ Yes, it's true,__ girl.

We'd like to say... to the new__ girl in town,

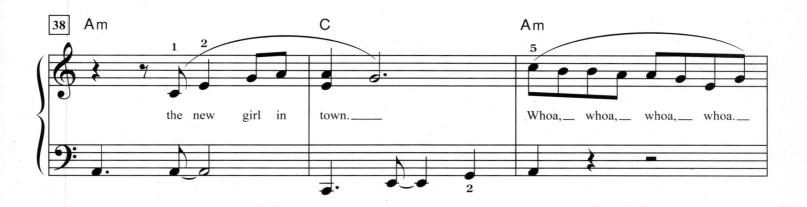

the new girl in town.__ Whoa,__ whoa,__ whoa,__ whoa.__

Freely

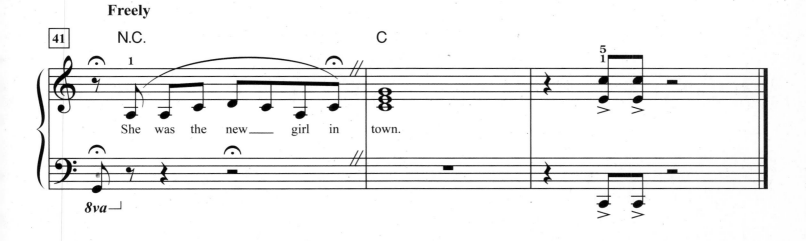

She was the new__ girl in town.

NEW SOUL

Words and Music by Yael Naïm and David Donatien
Arranged by Carol Matz

© 2007 LILI LOUISE MUSIQUE SARL (SACEM)
All Rights Administered by WB MUSIC CORP. (ASCAP)
All Rights Reserved

Chorus:

la la, la la la la la la, la la la la la, la la la, la la

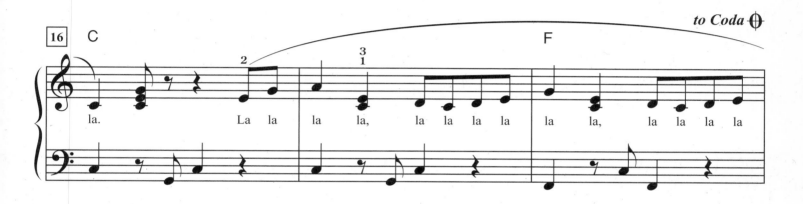

la. La la la la, la la la la la la, la la la la

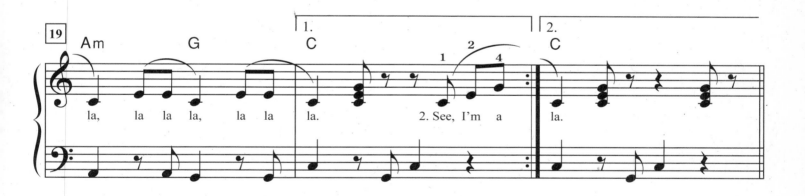

la, la la la, la la la. 2. See, I'm a la.

Bridge:

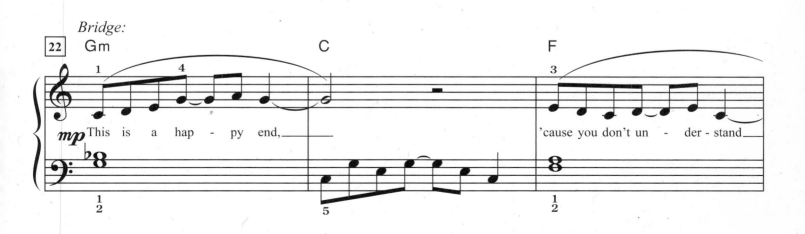

This is a hap - py end,＿＿ 'cause you don't un - der - stand＿＿

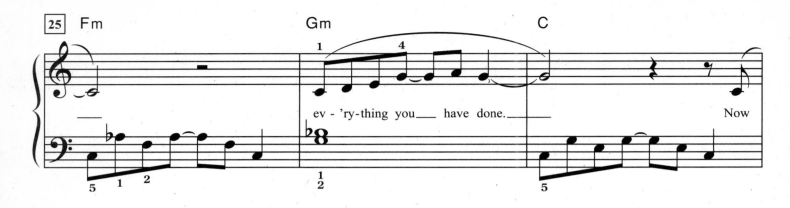

ev - 'ry-thing you___ have done.___ Now

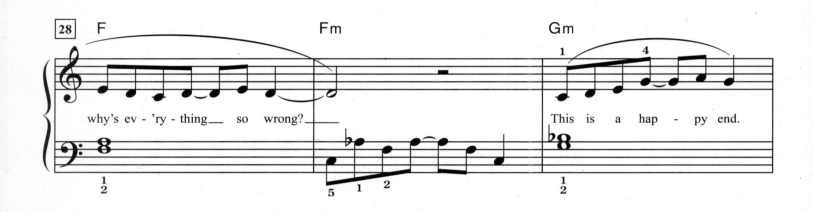

why's ev - 'ry - thing___ so wrong?___ This is a hap - py end.

Come and give me___ your hand. I'll take you far___ a - way. 3. I'm a

la, la la la, la la la. La la la la, la la la la

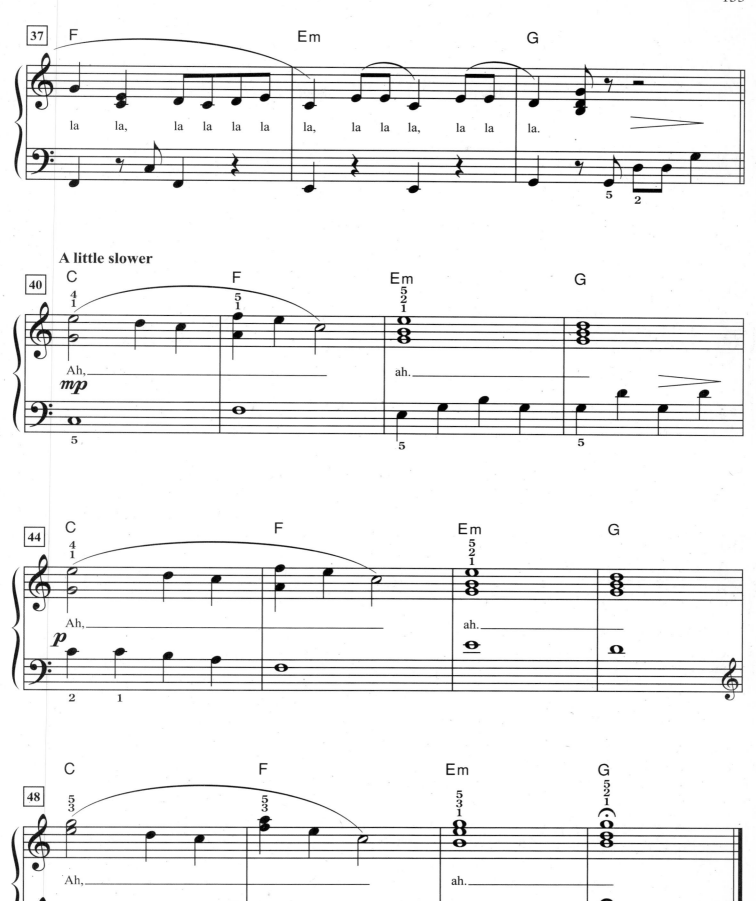

OVER THE RAINBOW

Music by Harold Arlen
Lyrics by E.Y. Harburg
Arranged by Carol Matz

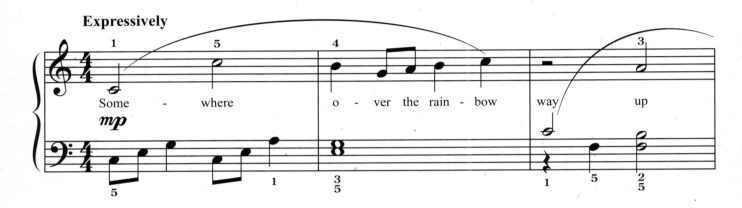

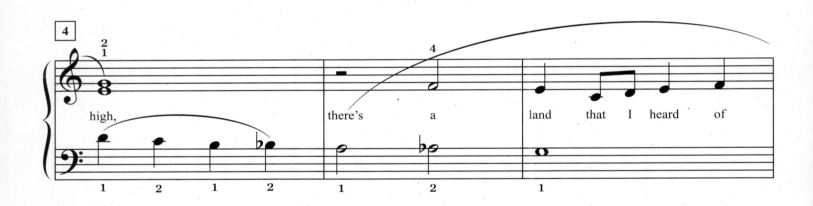

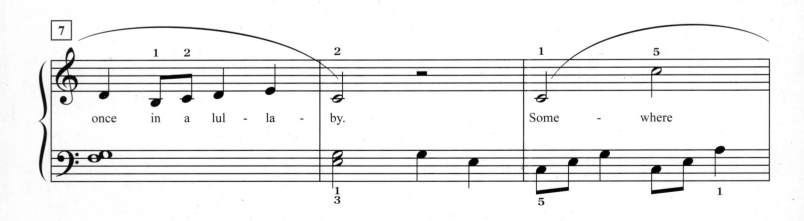

© 1938 (Renewed) METRO-GOLDWYN-MAYER INC. © 1939 (Renewed) EMI FEIST CATALOG INC.
All Rights Controlled and Administered by EMI FEIST CATALOG INC. (Publishing) and ALFRED PUBLISHING CO., INC. (Print)
All Rights Reserved

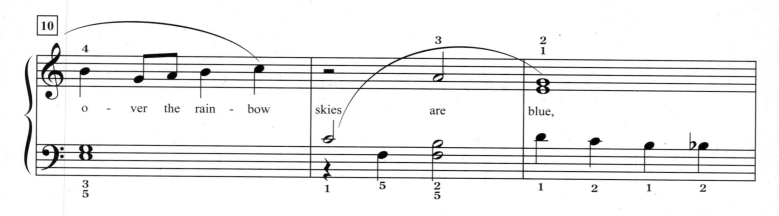

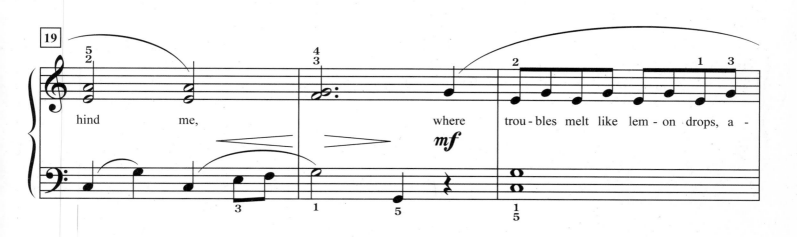

22

way a - bove the chim - ney tops, that's where you'll find me.

25 *a tempo*

Some - where o - ver the rain - bow blue - birds

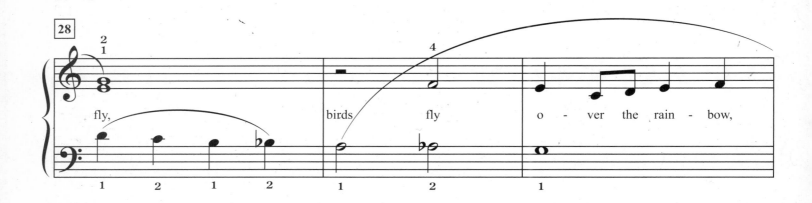

28

fly, birds fly o - ver the rain - bow,

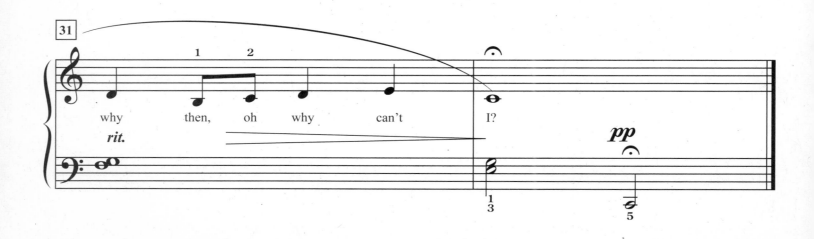

31

why then, oh why can't I?

rit.

pp

PARTY IN THE U.S.A.

Words and Music by
Claude Kelly, Lukasz Gottwald and Jessica Cornish
Arranged by Carol Matz

© 2009 WARNER-TAMERLANE PUBLISHING CORP., STUDIO BEAST MUSIC, KASZ MONEY PUBLISHING and SONY/ATV TUNES, LLC
All Rights on behalf of itself and STUDIO BEAST MUSIC Administered by WARNER-TAMERLANE PUBLISHING CORP.
All Rights Reserved

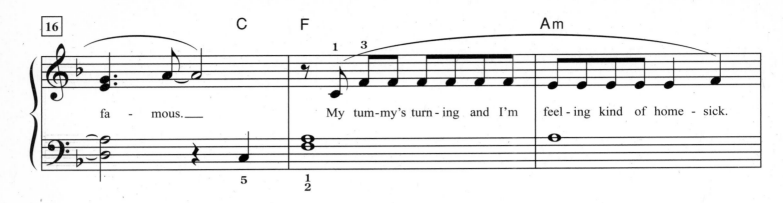

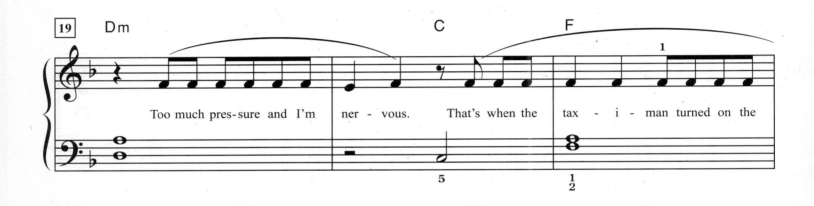

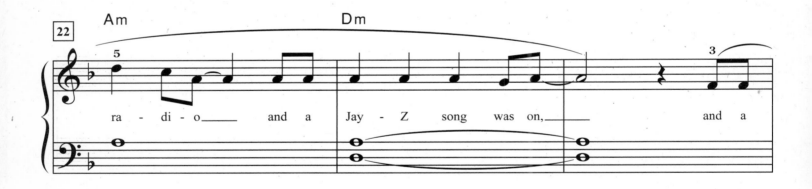

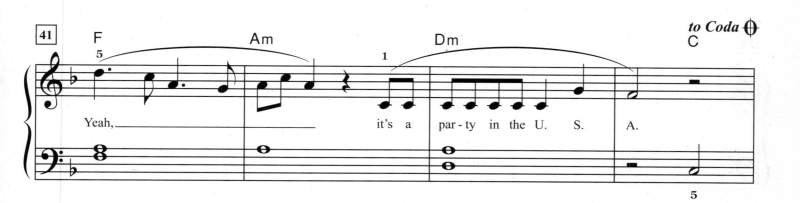

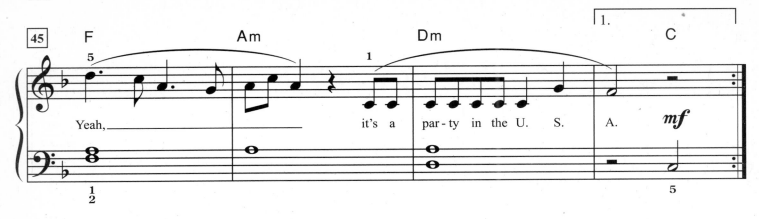

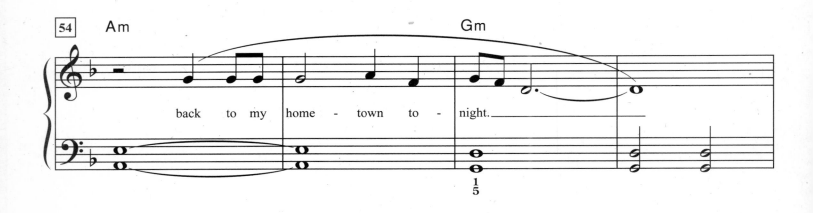

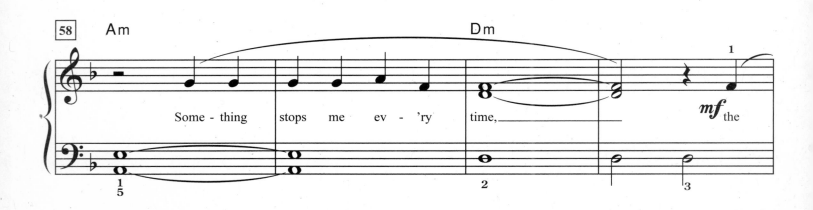

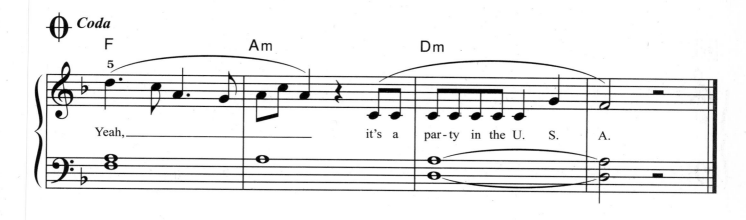

Verse 2:
Get to the club in my taxicab.
Everybody's looking at me now,
Like, "Who's that chick that's rockin' Kicks.
She's gotta be from out of town."
So hard with my girls not around me.
It's definitely not a Nashville party,
'Cause all I see are stilettos.
I guess I never got the memo.
My tummy's turning and I'm feeling kind of homesick.
Too much pressure and I'm nervous.
That's when the DJ dropped my favorite tune
And a Britney song was on,
And a Britney song was on,
And a Britney song was on.
(To Chorus:)

THE PINK PANTHER

(from *The Pink Panther*)

By Henry Mancini
Arranged by Carol Matz

© 1963 (Renewed) NORTHRIDGE MUSIC CO. and EMI U CATALOG INC.
Worldwide Print Rights Administered by ALFRED MUSIC PUBLISHING CO., INC.
All Rights Reserved

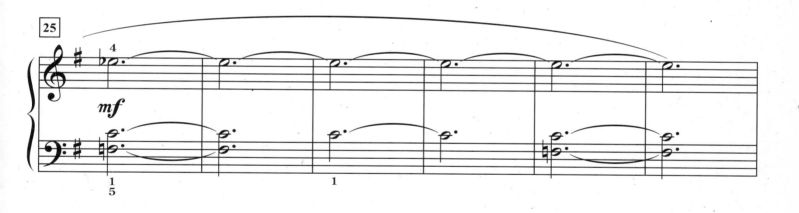

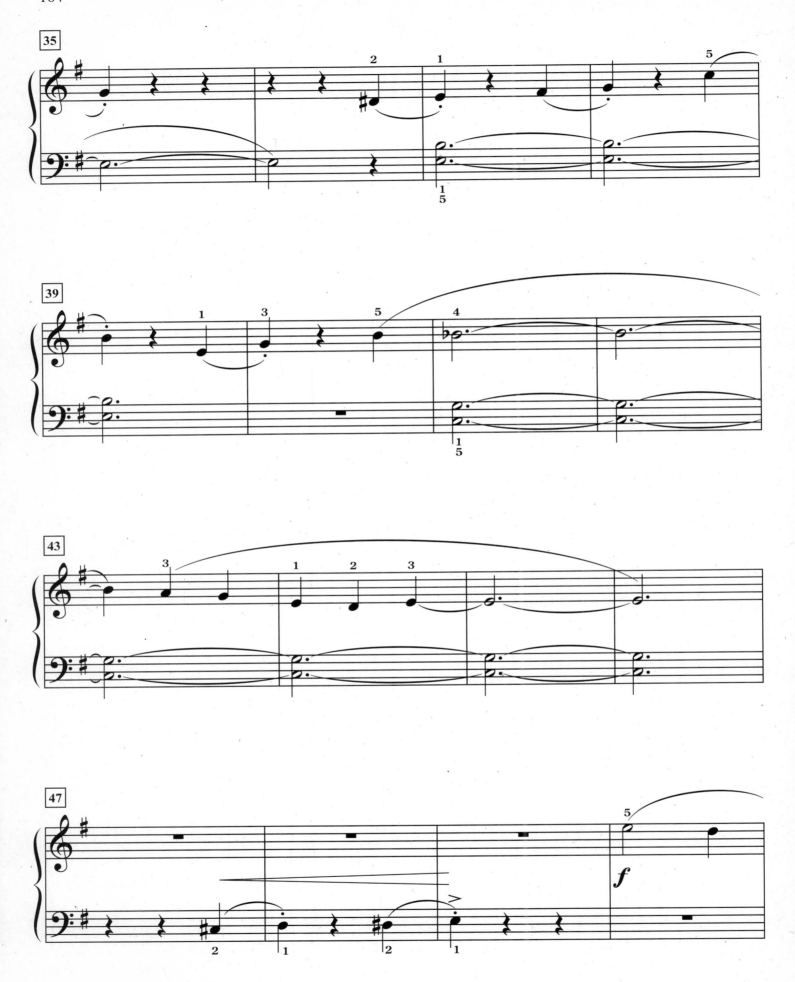

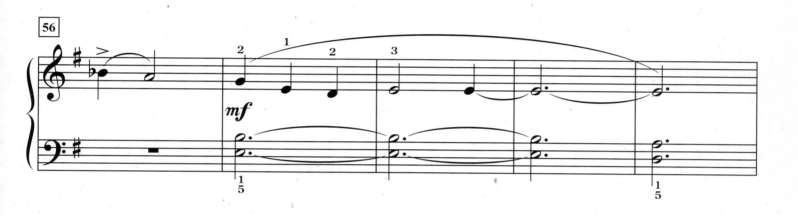

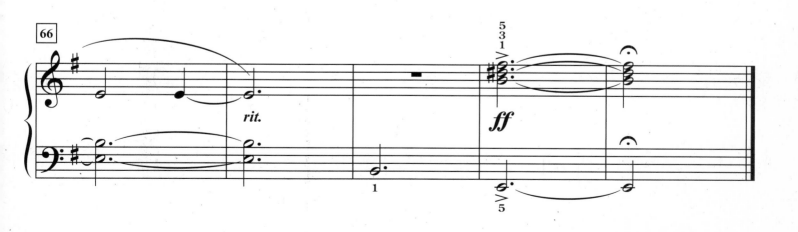

REMEMBER

(from *Troy*)

Lyrics by Cynthia Weil
Music by James Horner
Arranged by Carol Matz

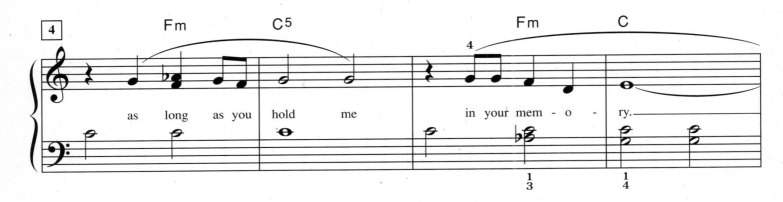

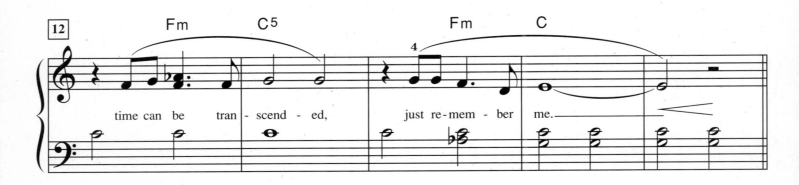

© 2004 WARNER-OLIVE MUSIC, LLC, HORNER MUSIC, WARNER-BARHAM MUSIC, LTD. and DYAD MUSIC, LTD.
All Rights Reserved

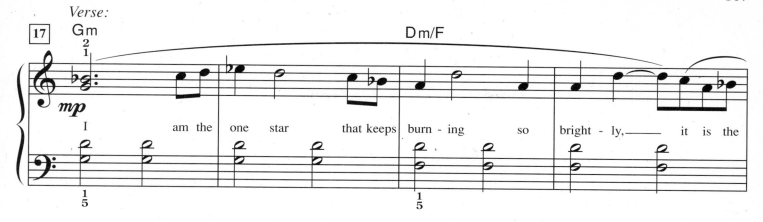

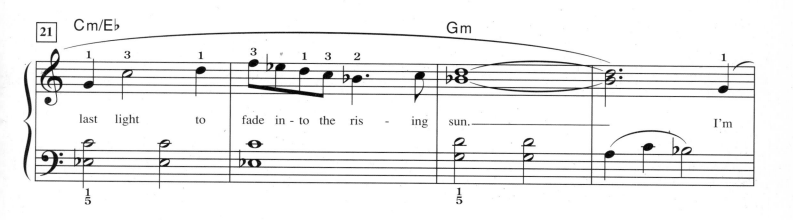

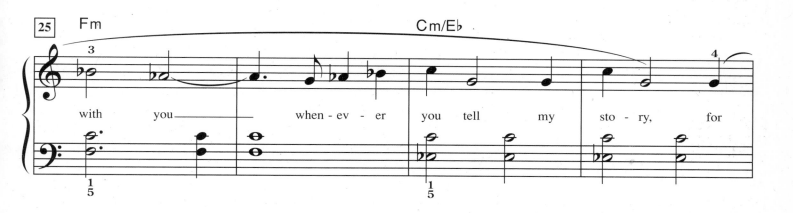

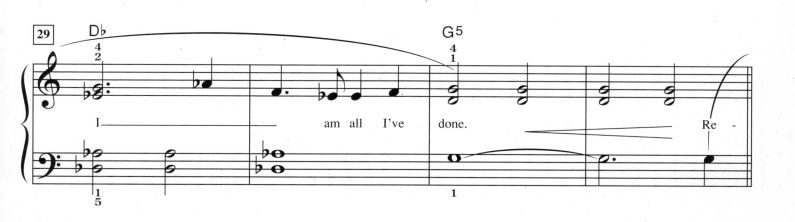

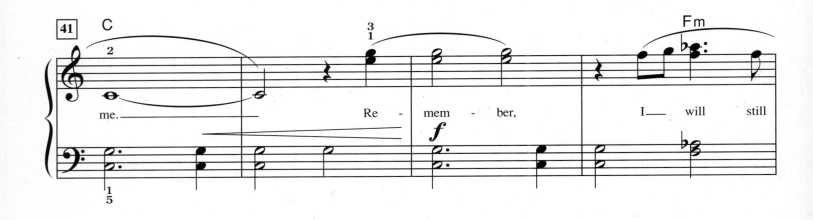

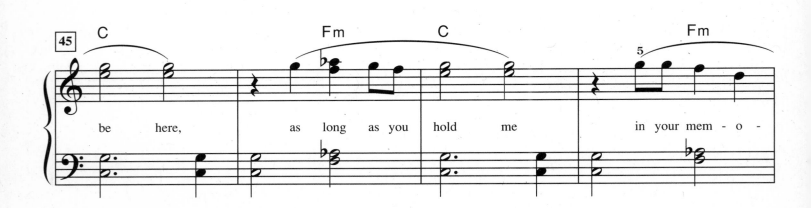

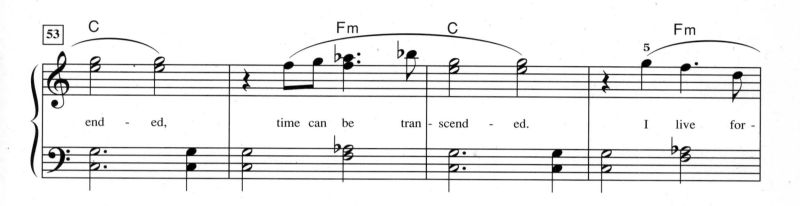

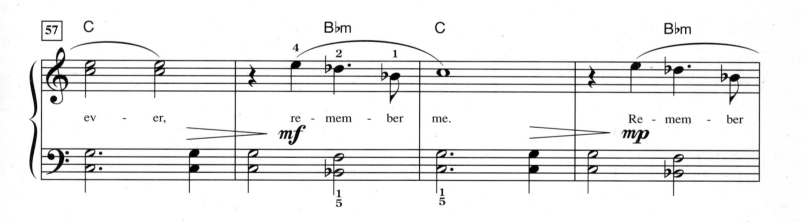

RAIDERS MARCH

(from *Indiana Jones and the Kingdom of the Crystal Skull*)

Music by JOHN WILLIAMS
Arranged by Carol Matz

Bright march

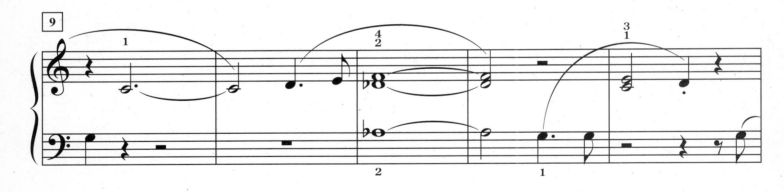

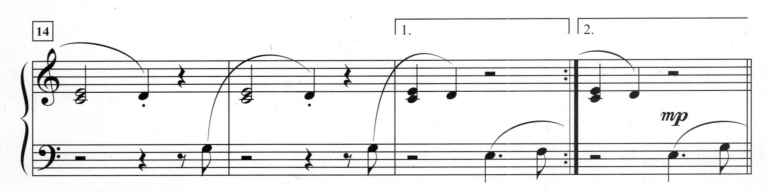

© 1981, 1984 BANTHA MUSIC (BMI)
All Rights Administered by WARNER-TAMERLANE PUBLISHING CORP. (BMI)
All Rights Reserved

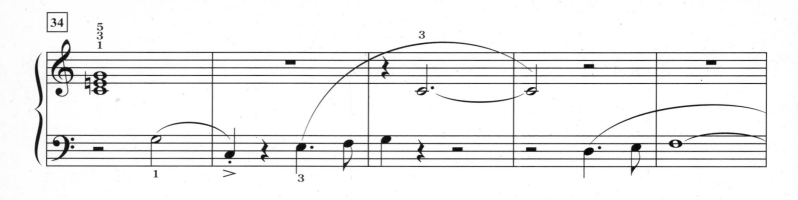

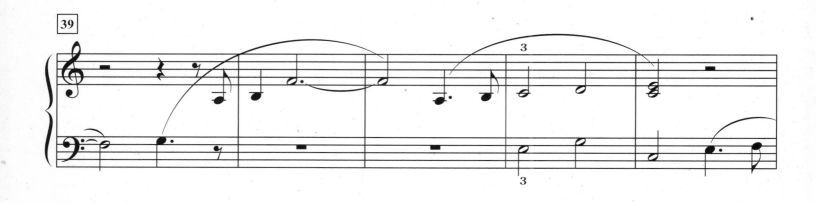

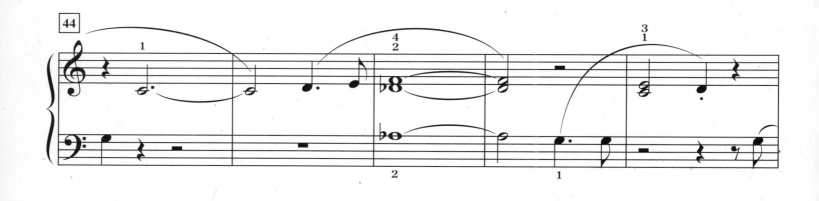

SOME HEARTS

Words and Music by Diane Warren
Arranged by Carol Matz

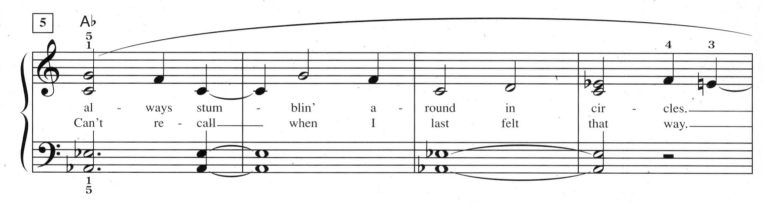

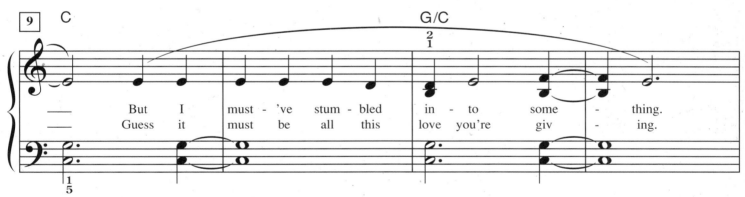

© 1989 REALSONGS
All Rights Reserved

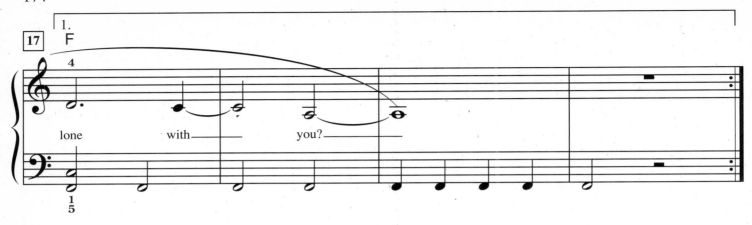

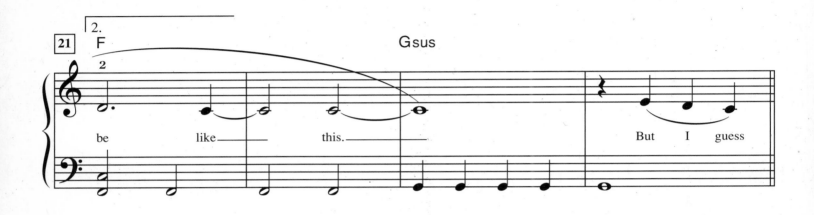

Chorus:

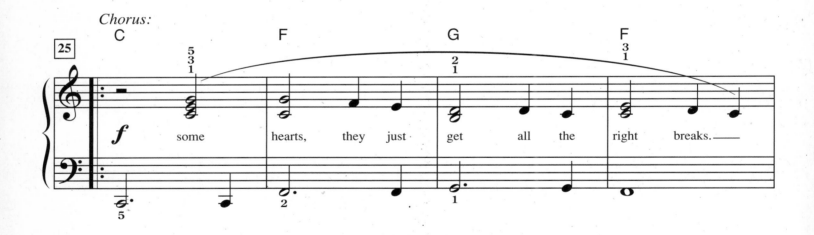

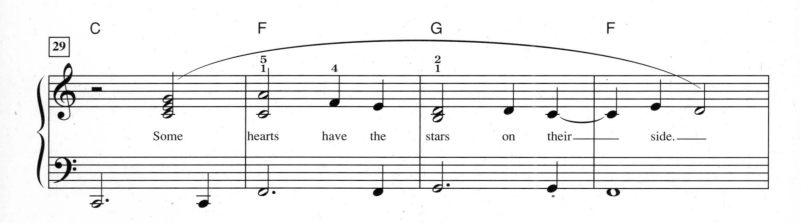

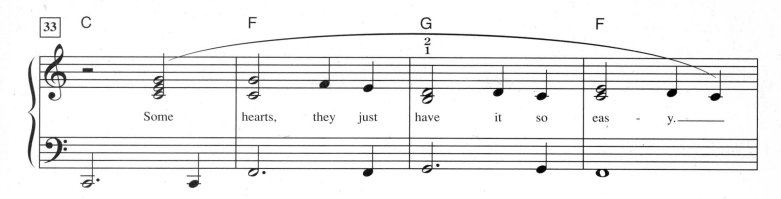

Some hearts, they just have it so eas - y.

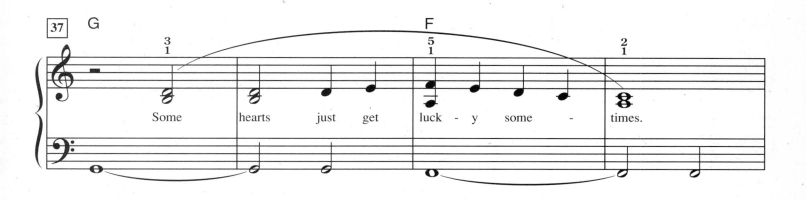

Some hearts just get luck - y some - times.

Some hearts just get luck - y,

1. luck - y some - times.

2. luck - y some - times.

THEME FROM *SUPERMAN*

(from *Superman Returns*)

Music by JOHN WILLIAMS
Arranged by Carol Matz

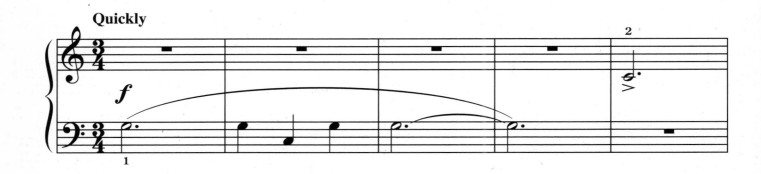

© 1978 (Renewed) WARNER-BARHAM MUSIC LLC (BMI)
All Rights Administered by SONGS OF UNIVERSAL, INC. (BMI)
Exclusive Worldwide Print Rights Administered by ALFRED MUSIC PUBLISHING CO., INC.
All Rights Reserved

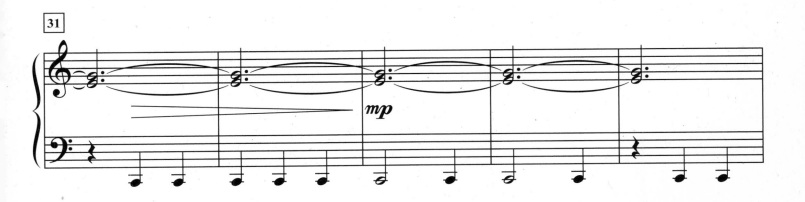

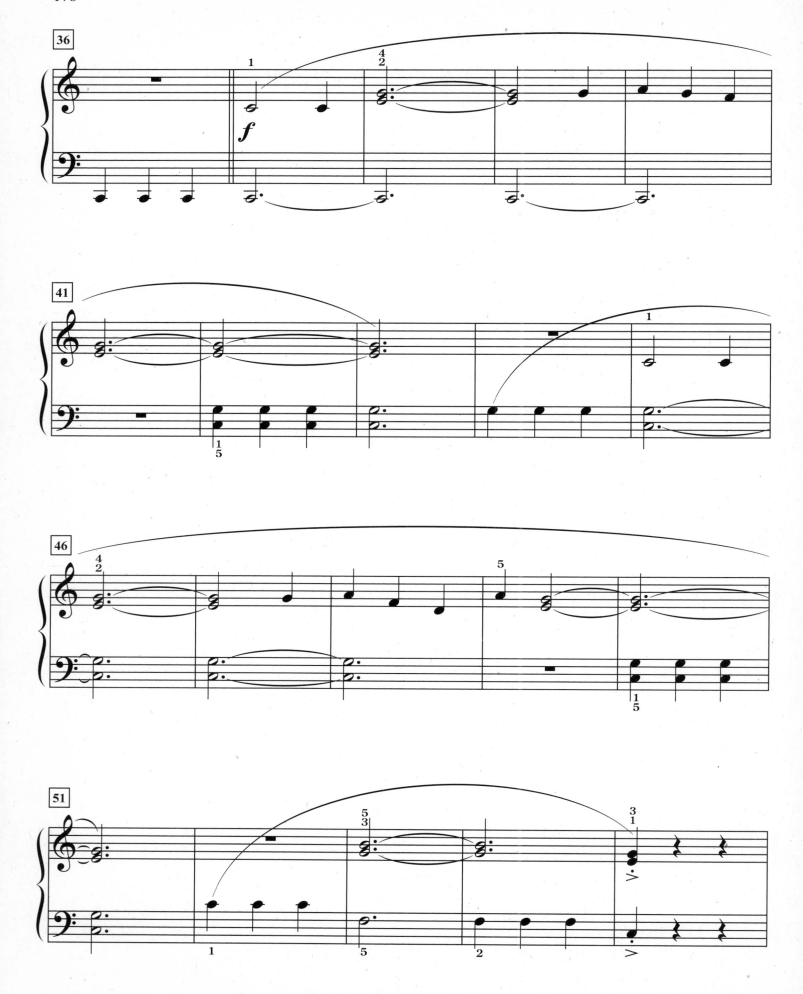

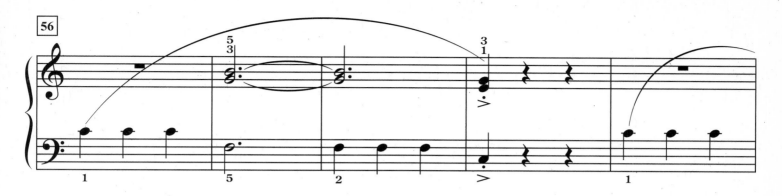

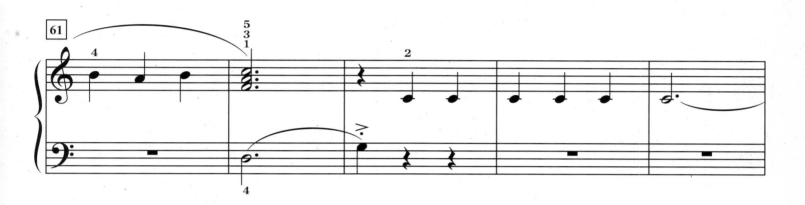

D.C. al Coda

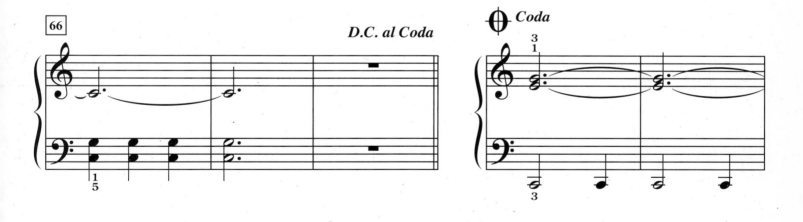

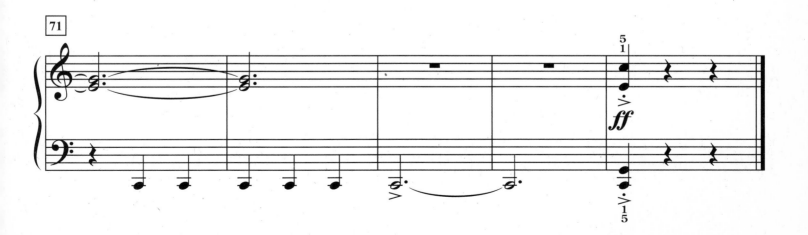

STAR WARS®

(Main Title)

By JOHN WILLIAMS
Arranged by Carol Matz

© 1977 (Renewed) WARNER-TAMERLANE PUBLISHING CORP. and BANTHA MUSIC
All Rights Administered by WARNER-TAMERLANE PUBLISHING CORP.
All Rights Reserved

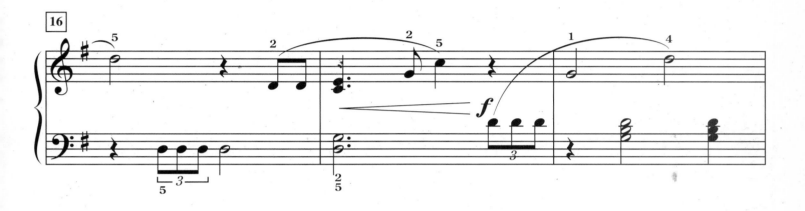

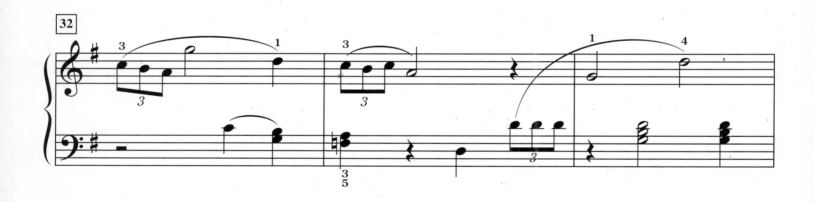

WAY BACK INTO LOVE

(from *Music and Lyrics*)

Words and Music by Adam Schlesinger
Arranged by Carol Matz

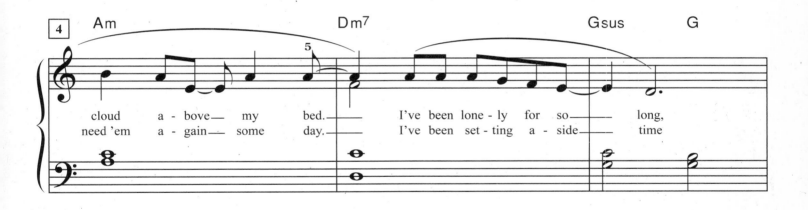

© 2007 VAGUELY FAMILIAR MUSIC and HAZEN MUSIC
All Rights for HAZEN MUSIC Administered by WB MUSIC CORP.
All Rights Reserved

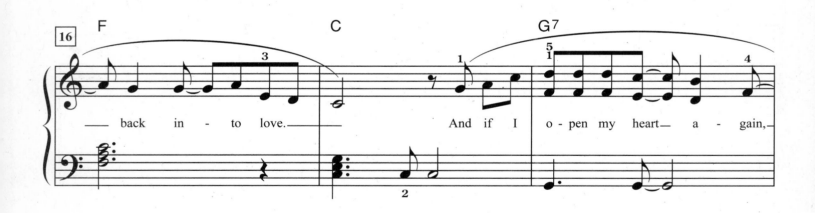

Verse:

There are mo-ments when I don't know if—— it's—— real,—— or if an-y-bod-y

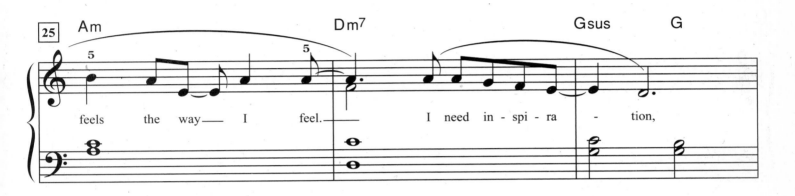

feels the way—— I feel.—— I need in-spi-ra ——— tion,

D.S. al Coda   **Coda**

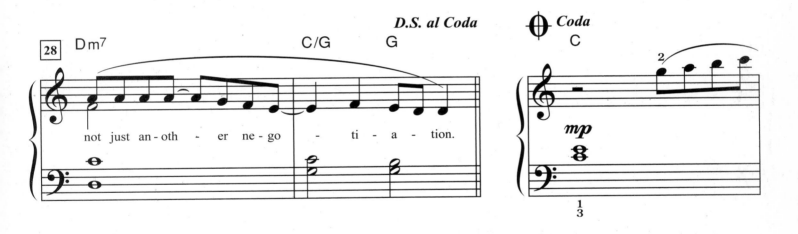

not just an-oth ——— er ne-go ——— ti - a - tion.

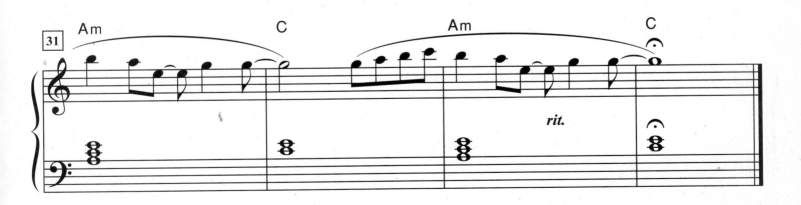

rit.

WILD HORSES

Words and Music by
Mick Jagger and Keith Richards
Arranged by Carol Matz

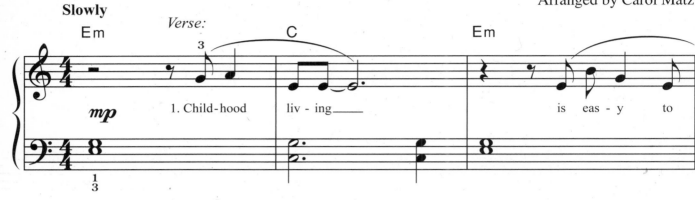

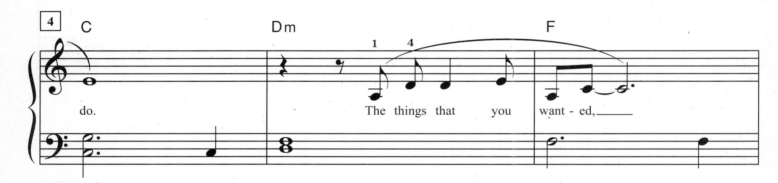

© 1970 (Renewed) ABKCO MUSIC INC., 85 Fifth Avenue, New York, NY 10003
All Rights Reserved

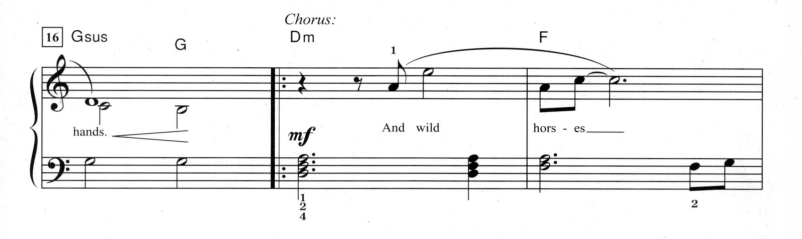

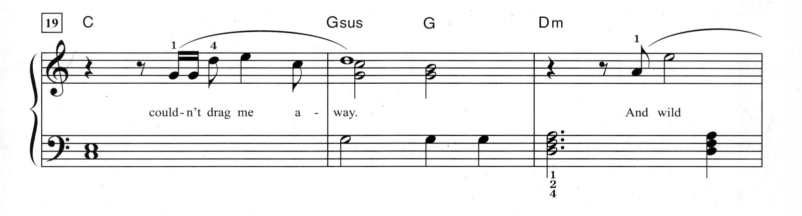

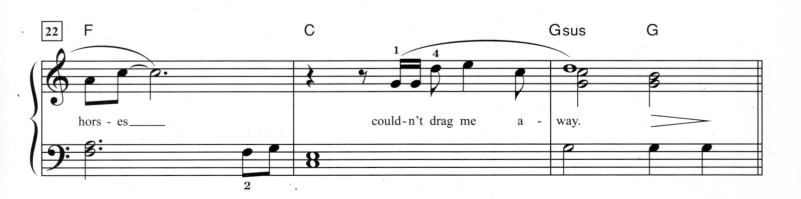

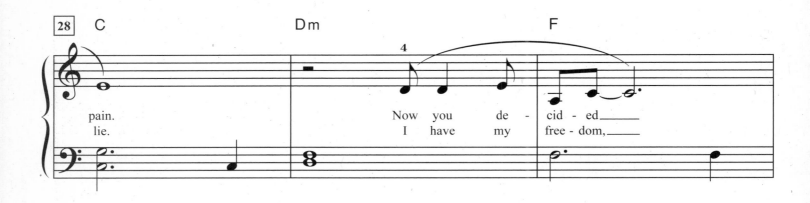

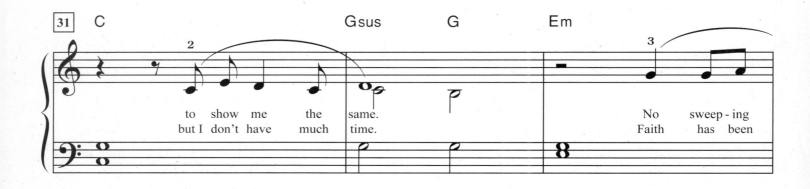

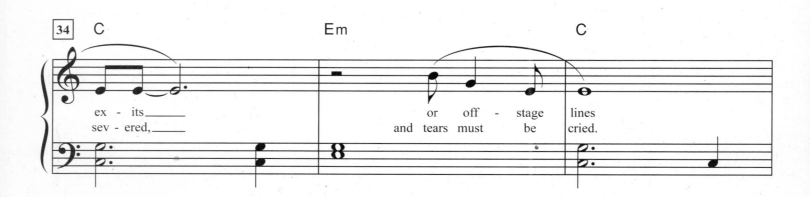

WORKING ON A DREAM

Words and Music by Bruce Springsteen
Arranged by Carol Matz

© 2008 BRUCE SPRINGSTEEN (ASCAP)
All Rights Reserved   Used By Permission

Chorus:

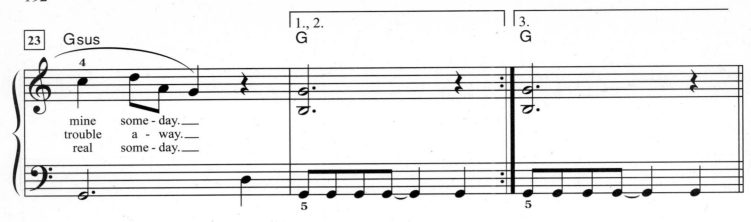

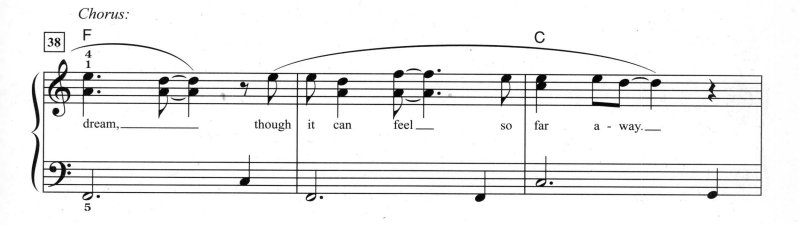

Chorus:

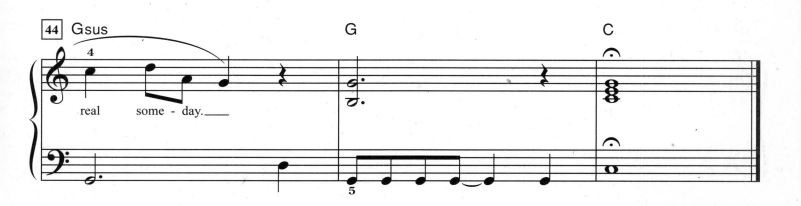

WONKA'S WELCOME SONG

(from *Charlie and the Chocolate Factory*)

Words by John August and Danny Elfman
Music by Danny Elfman
Arranged by Carol Matz

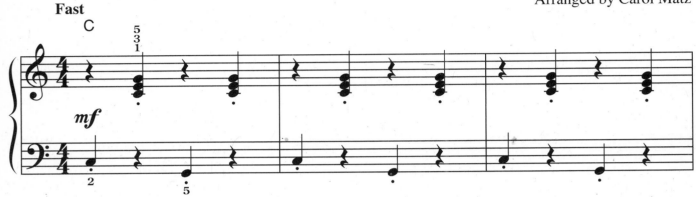

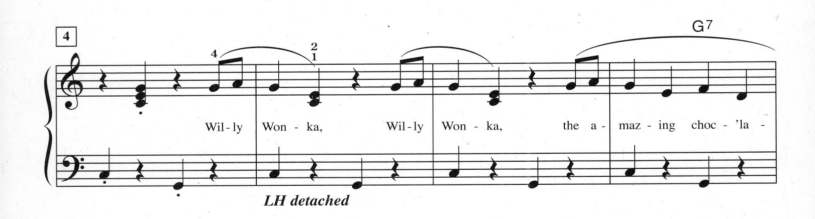

Wil - ly Won - ka, Wil - ly Won - ka, the a - maz - ing choc - 'la -

LH detached

tier. Wil - ly Won - ka, Wil - ly Won - ka, ev - 'ry - bod - y give a

© 2005 WARNER-BARHAM MUSIC, LLC (BMI) and MORTE PHARMECEUTICALS MUSIC CO. (BMI)
All Rights for WARNER-BARHAM MUSIC, LLC (BMI) SONGS OF UNIVERSAL, INC. (BMI)
Exclusive Worldwide Print Rights Administered by ALFRED MUSIC PUBLISHING CO., INC.
All Rights Reserved

195

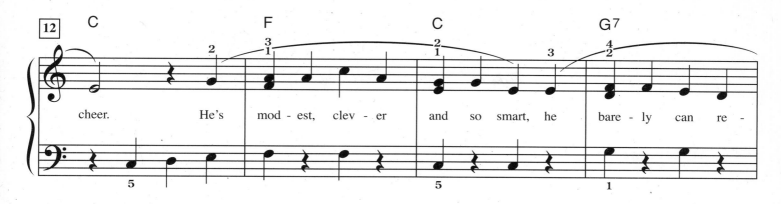

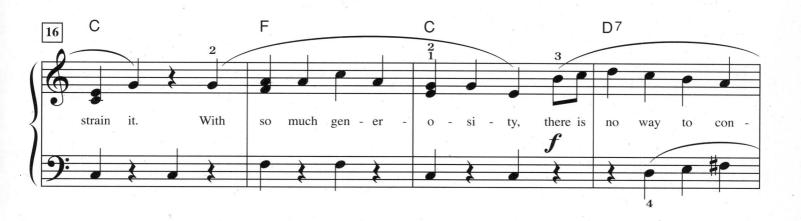

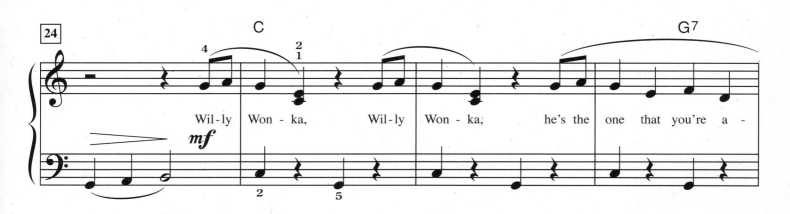

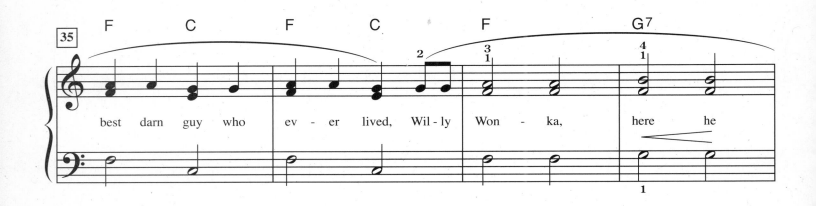

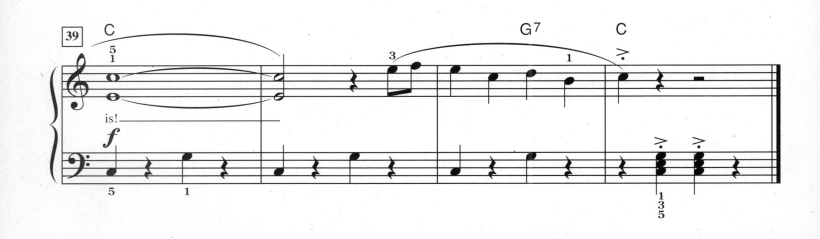